GREAT CREDIT
...Guaranteed!

**Improve your credit
in only 90 days...
or your money back!**

D1565310

ARNOLD S. GOLDSTEIN, PH.D.
Author of the bestselling 'So Sue Me!'

GREAT CREDIT GUARANTEE

We guarantee that this book will improve your credit to your complete satisfaction or we will fully refund the purchase price. This guarantee is made upon the following terms and conditions:

1. The book must be returned directly to the publisher at the below address. Do not return to retailer. This is a publisher's guarantee only.
2. The book must be returned in resalable condition and with the sales receipt within 90 days of purchase.
3. You shall be refunded the lesser of the publisher's list price or the actual purchase price. (Excluding shipping and handling, if any.)
4. Limit of one book returned, per purchaser.

Garrett Press, Inc.
368 South Military Trail
Deerfield Beach, FL 33442

Credit Guaranteed

By Arnold S. Goldstein, J.D., Ph.D.

Copyright © 2006, 2009 by Garrett Press, Inc.

Published by
Garrett Press, Inc.
368 South Military Trail
Deerfield Beach, FL 33442
Tel. 561-953-1322 • Fax 561-953-1940
E-mail: info@garrettpress.com • www.garrettpress.com

This publication is designed to provide accurate and authoritative information in regard to the subject matter covered. It is sold with the understanding that neither the publisher nor author is engaged in rendering legal, accounting, or other professional service. If legal advice or other expert assistance is required, the services of a competent professional should be sought. Neither the author nor the publisher shall have liability for any actions taken or not taken as a consequence of acting upon any information in this book.

Library of Congress Control Number: 2009927934

Goldstein, Arnold S.
    Great Credit Guaranteed/ Arnold S. Goldstein
    p.   cm.
    Includes bibliographical references and index.
    ISBN: 978-1-880539-87-3

        1. Credit bureaus - United States.
        2. Consumer credit - United States.
        3. Credit cards - United States. I. Title.

Printed in the United States of America

9 8 7 6 5 4 3 2 / D29

Quantity Discounts Available

ABOUT THE AUTHOR

Arnold S. Goldstein, Ph.D. has been called America's "Money Doctor." A nationally known credit and debt management strategist and asset protection attorney, he has helped thousands of clients resolve their credit and other financial problems. Other related books that he has authored include *The Complete Credit & Collection System*, *Getting Paid*, *Commercial Transactions Deskbook*, *So Sue Me!*, *Asset Protection Secrets*, *Turnaround*, *Debt Busters*, and *How To Settle With the IRS*. All are available from Garrett Press.

Goldstein's financial strategies have been featured or quoted in over 350 magazines, journals and newspapers, including *Inc., Bottom Line, Forbes, Business Week, Entrepreneur, Working Women, Success* and *Money*. Goldstein has also appeared on many radio and TV talk shows including the Today Show, CNN and CNBC. A popular speaker on credit and related subjects, his nationwide *Great Credit Guaranteed* workshops have attracted countless attendees. He has enjoyed a distinguished academic career as professor *emeritus* at Northeastern University and several other universities.

He holds two law degrees, an MBA and a Ph.D. (Northeastern University) and is a member of the Massachusetts Bar, Federal Bar, US Supreme Court Bar and numerous other professional and academic organizations. He lives in Delray Beach, Florida.

Dedicated to my wife Marlene, who always pays my bills on time and maintains my great credit score.

TABLE OF CONTENTS ■ ■ ■

How This book will Help You xi

1 The ABCs of Credit 15

2 How Good Is Your Credit? 39

3 How To Repair Bad Credit 61

4 How To Build Great Credit 93

5 How To Protect Your Credit 131

6 Credit Card Secrets 153

7 Credit Scams, Schemes and Traps 181

8 Sample Credit Letters 203

9 The Fair Credit Reporting Act 253

Index 335

HOW THIS BOOK WILL HELP YOU TO GET GREAT CREDIT

Great credit is essential today. Without great credit you cannot get a mortgage, finance a car, obtain a credit card or even charge a good meal at a fine restaurant. Whatever credit you can get you will pay a premium for. Nearly everything you buy on credit will be more costly.

America is a credit society. We buy nearly everything on credit. Without credit, you are forced to pay as you go. You can buy only what you can immediately pay for. If that's your plight, *Great Credit Guaranteed* can help you change your life.

- ■ If you have *no* credit, it will show you how to establish credit.

- ■ If you have *bad* credit, it will show you how to turn it into good credit.

- ■ If you have *good* credit, it will show you how to develop *great* credit.

- ■ If you already have great credit, it will show you how to use it more intelligently, avoid those nasty credit scams and save money on your credit transactions.

Great credit just doesn't happen. Building great credit takes time and persistence. Most of all, it takes know-how. That's where *Great Credit Guaranteed* is invaluable. It explains everything you must know to repair, build, protect and use your credit. Here are the hundreds of little known secrets that you must know to wisely use credit - the answers you need to survive and thrive in our credit system. But there is more. Presented in an easy-to-understand Q & A format, *Great Credit Guaranteed* will also show you how to:

- ■ Obtain and evaluate your credit report - as others check your credit.

- ■ Eliminate every negative mark that destroys credit.

- ■ Add positive credit marks to your credit report and build a high credit score.

- ■ Unburden yourself from overwhelming credit card debt.

- ■ Manage your credit more wisely.

- ■ Get credit on the best terms for those essential but expensive purchases a car, home mortgage, college education, etc.

- ■ Exploit your great credit to build wealth faster.

- ■ Avoid costly credit scams, schemes and traps.

- ■ Save money on every credit purchase.
  . . . and much more.

Thousands of people from every walk of life have successfully applied my 'great credit' secrets. Some never had good credit. Others had their good credit ruined by unavoidable financial problems. Still others had good credit but needed more credit. Many were entrepreneurs who wanted credit for their business. No matter who you are, and whatever your present credit situation may be – you can improve your credit. *Great Credit Guaranteed* gives you the blueprint and *guarantees* the results!

If you closely follow my credit-building strategies, your credit *will* improve! That is why my publisher can confidently offer you a 100 percent money-back guarantee. If you are not completely satisfied with your credit after you apply my credit building techniques, please return the book to the publisher and you'll be refunded every penny you paid for the book. (See guarantee conditions in the front of this book.) What can be fairer? I am equally confident that Great *Credit Guaranteed* will work wonders for your credit rating for you just as it has for tens of thousands of others who have already used my guaranteed credit program with consistent success. I receive their grateful comments by phone, letter and directly from attendees at my nationwide *Great Credit Guaranteed* seminars.

The credit improvement methods I reveal to you aren't textbook theory. They result from the trial by fire that comes from my 25 years experience helping people cope with their credit problems. As I have learned, you will learn everything you must know about our credit system and how you can legally exploit the system to your maximum advantage. That is this book's objective.

What You Will Find In Great Credit Guaranteed

Great Credit Guaranteed begins with an in-depth explanation of how our credit system operates, and the key role the credit bureaus play in compiling and reporting credit. You will learn how these bureaus really function as well as who is legally entitled to get credit information about you. You will then see how to obtain and read your own credit report. Then we proceed step-by-step through the fundamentals of credit repair which should help you to repair most – if not every – credit problem. To combat those more stubborn credit problems, you will also see advanced strategies to resolve credit problems due to tax liens, foreclosures, repossessions, bankruptcy and judgments.

With your credit score improved, you will find the powerful and proven techniques to build your credit score. I then uncover the secrets to obtain and wisely use credit cards.

But that's only the beginning. *Great Credit Guaranteed* ensures that as a credit consumer you will never again be victimized as we highlight the consumer protection laws that protect your credit rights and explain the obligations of creditors and credit bureaus to you.

Yes, it's all here. And in addition to giving you clear, step-by-step strategies to repair, restore and rebuild your credit, I also give you over forty sample letters to protect your rights in virtually every credit situation. Adapt or customize these letters and correspondence to fit your own special situation.

A final note: This book has not been written to help you abuse the credit system, commit fraud or violate the rights of creditors. It is designed to give you every legal tool you need to protect your credit rights and use them for your maximum protection.

So let's get *you* on the road to great credit!

Arnold S. Goldstein, Ph.D.
Boca Raton, Flordia

ONE

THE ABC's OF CREDIT 1

How often have you heard someone boast "I pay cash for everything," or "I never borrowed a dime in my life?" Years ago we admired this 'pay-as-you-go' philosophy. It suggested that you had the income and cash to buy whatever you wanted. With a solid income and sound financial management you could realize the American dream.

Sadly, this is no longer true. We now live in a credit society. Without good credit you cannot finance a decent car, take a vacation, get a home mortgage, start a business or even buy an expensive dinner.

Everything is changing. Economies. Technologies. Business practices. We have become transformed into a virtual cashless society. Cash is no longer king. The crown goes to good credit. The typical consumer no longer pays cash for their basic necessities, let alone their more expensive purchases. Much of what you need must be financed. This takes great credit.

Great credit, even when unessential, is certainly convenient. Why walk around with large amounts of cash? Nor will everyone accept your check. Great credit, on the other hand, is invisible, weighs nothing and managed properly, is instantly available. You can impulse buy. Your purchases are no longer limited to the cash in your pocket or bank account. Great credit, in a word, is power!

Great credit measures your financial worth. More importantly, it also reflects your financial progress, character, and how others view your future prospects. Great credit also gives you financial leverage. Lenders consider great credit as its own form of collateral, and they finance you based upon that reality. Great credit also is confidence – the confidence others have in you – and a way to build your own self-confidence. With great credit you can plan, take risks and compete more effectively. This is good for both you and society. In fact, our society could not function efficiently without credit. Industry would grind to a halt and we would return to a feudal barter system. With great credit you can claim your own stake in the American dream.

Everyone needs great credit. If you are young, mastering credit management can be your foundation to future wealth. Great credit will let you harness other people's money and talent. The financial advantage you gain will remain yours for the rest of your life. If you are older, great credit equates to a measure of financial security.

What is credit?

Credit is simply a system where you can 'buy now, pay later.' With credit you can enjoy a purchase today and pay for it later – or over time. There are many different credit arrangements available today – credit cards, personal loans, home mortgages, store charge accounts, educational loans, lines of credit, etc. These are only a few of hundreds of examples.

How do I determine the cost of credit?

You must always measure and compare the costs of credit. And since the costs of credit can vary considerably, you must be an informed credit consumer.

The Federal Truth-In-Lending Act requires creditors to provide you basic information about the costs of credit. This information will include the finance charge, amount financed and annual percentage rate (APR).

Whenever you apply for open-end credit (merchants accounts, bankcards, etc.), you must also be told the method of calculating the finance charges, and when the finance charges accrue. You should receive this information in writing before you sign any credit agreement. Much of this information must also be disclosed in any advertisement that mentions credit.

How important is it to shop for the best credit terms?

It's critical. Most people don't shop for credit as they should. They may, for example, comparison price a new car, but how many car buyers closely compare finance charges on their auto purchase? Few.

With the great number of credit arrangements available today, it is important to compare options – including whether you can get better financing on your outstanding credit arrangements.

How common are credit problems?

There are no precise statistics, but obviously plenty of folks have credit problems. So, if you have less than perfect credit you are not alone. Unfortunately, too many individuals and companies have credit or debt problems. The poor economy is one reason. Unemployment also affects millions. Nor can we overlook that nearly two million Americans file bankruptcy each year for a wide variety of reasons.

Would this book be important to me if I already have good credit?

Absolutely. Because your goal then is to turn good credit into great credit – or the highest credit rating possible. With the highest credit rating you can get more credit (if and when you need it), and also get credit on the best terms – which will save you money.

Why do so many people have faulty credit?

There are two basic reasons for faulty credit: First, too few people pay enough attention to their credit score because they generally get whatever credit they request (although seldom on the best terms). Secondly, too few credit consumers know their rights, or they fail to assert their legal rights as credit consumers.

Can you really repair 'bad' credit?

Absolutely. Not only can you, but it is essential that you do. No matter how poor your current credit rating, you can restore and improve your credit score until you obtain an excellent credit rating. It may take a year or two (or less if you now have fair credit), but once you develop good credit habits you should eventually be able to get whatever credit you reasonably need.

What are the most common reasons for poor credit?

Most credit problems fall within two categories: In the first group are those who have never established good credit, and in the second group, are those who had their credit damaged. Bad credit can happen for any number of reasons: Poor money management, no financial discipline, divorce, business failure, job loss, unexpected medical bills, falling victim to financial scams, etc. There are many other reasons someone may lose their good credit. For example, poor credit also increasingly results from identity theft and errors by the credit reporting bureaus.

What are the different types of credit?

While there are many different ways to borrow money, there are only four types of credit: 1) Secured credit; 2) unsecured credit; 3) installment credit; and 4) non-installment credit.

What is the difference between secured and unsecured credit?

Secured credit is backed by collateral. You pledge an asset to the lender and if you fail to repay, the lender may sell the collateral. Collateral may be your car, jewelry, real estate, a passbook savings account or any other asset that you and the lender agree upon. Because you have pledged collateral, the lender has less risk, and therefore secured credit is often the easiest credit to obtain. A home mortgage or auto loan are the most common examples of secured credit.

With unsecured credit the lender extends you credit based upon your ability and willingness to repay. This is evidenced by your credit history. You do not pledge collateral, and because no collateral is pledged, the lender has greater risk of loss if you do not pay. Therefore, the lender must have more confidence in your ability and willingness to pay the debt. Unsecured credit is chiefly granted upon your credit history and current financial condition. If you default, the lender must go to court to sue, and only after the creditor obtains a judgment can it seize your assets to recover its money.

How does installment credit differ from non-installment credit?

Installment credit can be either secured or unsecured. Installment debt is repaid in periodic payments or installments over a specified time. One variation of this type of credit is when each payment automatically makes available an equal amount of new credit. This is sometimes called 'open-end' or revolving credit. For example, a revolving charge account with a department store may give you a credit limit that automatically renews as you pay. Other common examples of installment loans are automobile, educational and personal loans.

If you pay late, you are charged a late fee. More importantly, defaults or late payments may become negative marks on your credit report.

Non-installment credit can be secured or unsecured. It is paid in one payment and by a specified date. A statement 'payable in full upon receipt' is an example of non-installment credit. Telephone bills and doctors' statements are also common examples of non-installment credit.

What laws protect me as a credit consumer?

It is vital to understand your legal rights as a credit consumer. The most important law is the Consumer Credit Protection Act (CCPA), enacted by Congress to protect consumers from unfair credit practices. This law also regulates credit reporting bureaus, collection agencies and creditors, and further prevents credit discrimination as well as providing many other consumer credit protections.

The Consumer Credit Protection Act is divided into four important sections (which we further cover within this book): 1) The Fair Credit Reporting Act (FCRA), 2) The Fair Credit Billing Act, 3) The Fair Debt Collection Practices Act (FDCA), and 4) The Equal Credit Opportunity Act (ECOA).

The Fair Credit Reporting Act defines the responsibilities of creditors and credit reporting bureaus when dealing with credit consumers. The FCRA ensures that credit consumers have the right to their credit file, and it guarantees the privacy of that information as well. Your rights as a credit consumer under the FCRA also include:

- Your right to access all credit information about you – by phone, mail, or in person (except medical information) that is contained in your credit file at any consumer reporting bureau.

- Your right to have a credit reporting bureau disclose to you the nature, substance and sources of its information.

- Your right – if you have been denied credit, employment or insurance because of a credit report – to know the name of the bureau that issued that report.

■ Your right – if you have been denied credit within the past 30 days, in whole or in part, as a result of a credit report issued by a credit reporting bureau – to obtain a free copy of that credit report.

■ Your right to appear in person at the credit bureau to review your credit file.

■ Your right to dispute information in your credit report, and to have that dispute investigated by the credit bureau within 30 days.

■ Your right to have inaccurate or erroneous information deleted from your credit file.

■ Your right to have the credit bureau delete from your credit files any information that it cannot verify within 30 days.

■ Your right to have the credit bureau update information to anyone who has received your credit file.

■ Your right to know the identity of anyone who has requested a copy of your credit report within the past 6 months.

■ Your right to know the names of everyone who has been furnished your credit report within the past 2 years.

■ Your right to include a brief consumer statement to your credit report.

■ Your right to have negative credit information deleted from your credit report after the statutory time period for reporting such information has expired.

- Your right to sue a credit reporting agency for violations of law.

- Your right to be notified by anyone requesting an investigative consumer report on you – as well as the nature and substance of the investigation.

How does the Fair Credit Billing Act protect me as a credit consumer?

The Fair Credit Billing Act protects credit consumers against inaccurate and unfair credit billing and credit card practices. Your rights as a consumer under this law are:

- Your right to challenge, in writing, any creditor's billing statement or the amount of that billing statement.

- Your right to have the creditor respond within 30 days from their receipt of your notice.

- Your right to have a creditor either correct the account or show proof that the account has been investigated and verified within 90 days of notice.

- Your right to have the creditor supply you with proof that your account has been corrected or proof that your debt was verified within 90 days of notice.

- Your right, once you notify a creditor that you dispute a bill, not to have your account reported as delinquent for 100 days after receiving notice from you of the dispute.

- Your right, if the account remains disputed after the lapsed statutory time, to force the creditor to report the account 'in dispute.'

- Your right to have that creditor furnish you with the name and address of every party to whom the report was furnished that contains the disputed account entry.

- Your right to have any settlement of an account reported to third parties to whom reports were originally furnished.

- Your right to have any bill which may incur a finance charge, mailed to you at least 14 days before the due date.

- Your right to a refund or credit for overpayments.

- Your right not to be required to purchase additional 'tie-in' services to obtain a credit card.

What are the important provisions of the Fair Debt Collection Practice?

The Fair Debt Collection Practices Act does not directly deal with credit, but rather specifies the permissible practices by creditors when dealing with debtors. The Fair Debt Collection Practices Act protects consumers from unfair and deceptive debt collection practices. Your rights as a consumer under this law are:

- Your right not to be abused, harassed, or deceived by debt collectors.

- Your right not to be contacted by any debt collector before 8 a.m. or after 9 p.m.

- Your right to have a debt collector identify himself when contacting you.

- Your right not to have a debt collector misrepresent himself.

- Your right – should a debt collector communicate with a third party about you – not to have the collector mention your debt, but only seek information concerning your location. Moreover, the creditor may not communicate with any such person more than once – unless requested to do so.

- Your right not to have a debt collector communicate by postcard.

- Your right not to have a debt collector use any symbol on an envelope or telegram that indicates or refers to debt collection.

- Your right – if the debt collector has reason to believe you are represented by an attorney – not to communicate with any other person, and only communicate with you through your attorney.

- Your right – if your employer forbids such communication – to forbid a debt collector from communicating with you at work.

- Your right to inform the debt collector in writing to cease all further communication, and that it must do so after informing you of any further actions to be taken.

- Your right not to be threatened with violence to your person or property.

- Your right not to have your name published as a debtor.

- Your right not to have your debt advertised as available for sale.

- Your right not to be subject to obscene or profane language.

- Your right not to have a debt collector harass you by telephone.

- Your right not to have a debt collector falsely identify himself as employed by any branch of the federal or state government.

- Your right not to have a debt collector falsely identify himself as an attorney.

- Your right not to have a debt collector falsely imply that you or your property will be subject to arrest, imprisonment, seizure, garnishment, or attachment.

- Your right to notify the debt collector within the statutory 30-day period, in writing, that you dispute the debt or request the name and address of the original creditor. Upon such notification, the collector must cease all debt collection activities against you pending verification of the debt. Proof of verification must be mailed to you by the debt collector.

- Your right to sue a debt collector for actual and punitive damages resulting from violation of this act.

What does the Equal Credit Opportunity Act cover?

The Equal Credit Opportunity Act prohibits credit discrimination on the basis of race, color, religion, national origin, sex, or marital status. Nor may you be denied credit because you are on public assistance or because you have exercised your rights under the Consumer Credit Protection Act. Your rights as a consumer under this law are:

■ Your right – if you are denied credit or have your credit revoked – to be informed by the creditor, in writing, of the specific reason for the denial.

■ Your right to have the creditor supply the in-formation within 90 days of any written request for same.

■ Your right to sue in the federal courts, any credit-or who violates this law for actual and punitive damages.

■ Your right to join in a class action lawsuit against the debt collector.

■ Your right to sue for violations under the Civil Rights Act.

Where can I find more information about these laws?

Visit my website *www.assetprotectionattorneys.com* or contact the FTC. Of course, these laws are also covered in much greater detail throughout this book. Remember, these laws are for your protection, so keep in mind their key provisions.

If my rights as a credit consumer are violated, are my remedies limited to those under the FCRA?

Not necessarily. Your state probably has its own credit laws, and many states impose harsher penalties than those under the FCRA. If your state has its own credit laws, you can also file legal action in your state courts.

When should I use credit and when should I pay cash?

The axiom is that when you can afford it, it is usually wiser to pay cash for your purchases. However, that is not always possible, and you may probably need credit:

- To buy a home, auto or some other expensive purchases for which you do not have sufficient cash.

- When your purchase will return to you more money than the cost of financing credit (interest).

- When you need an essential item but do not have available cash.

- When you need credit for travel (hotels, rental cars, etc.).

- When you want the transaction to come under the consumer protection provisions of the Federal Fair Credit Billing Act.

- When you want to buy online.

- When emergencies arise for which you have insufficient cash.

How do I find my best source for loans?

The main factor to consider is your creditor's lending criteria. Lenders have different criteria. Some only lend to existing customers, or to those with specific income levels or other credit standards. Most importantly, ask whether the lender makes the type loan you are interested in as credit is a highly specialized industry.

What are the obligations of a prospective creditor when I apply for credit?

When you apply for credit, the Federal Equal Credit Opportunity Act requires the creditor to act on your application within 30 days.

If you are denied credit (or granted less credit than requested), the creditor must either give you the reason for the decision or advise you that you have the right to know the reason. If the rejection letter does not give you the reason for credit declination, you may request this information in writing within 60 days.

What creditors must comply with the Equal Credit Opportunity Act?

The ECOA applies to any creditor who routinely extends credit or who participates in the credit-granting decision. This extends to banks, merchants, credit card companies and similar credit-issuing organizations as well as those who routinely arrange financing (real estate or mortgage brokers, etc.).

I have been told that I need credit to build credit. Is that true?

Yes. Surprisingly, some people do pay cash for everything, and as a result they have no credit history. Without a credit history there is no way for a prospective creditor to know whether they will pay if they are granted credit. So everyone needs at least several credit transactions on file to establish their credit worthiness.

Can you give me a fast overview of how I would repair or build my credit?

Every credit repair program has two major objectives: 1) Remove every negative mark from your credit report. 2) Add as many positive marks as possible to your credit report. Later chapters will show you how to achieve this.

How does our credit system work?

A network of credit reporting agencies track the credit of every American. They are the guardians of our credit system. Whenever you apply for credit, the prospective creditor will first check your credit with one or more of these credit bureaus.

There are nearly 2,000 credit agencies throughout the United States; however, only three national bureaus centralize America's credit information – Experian, TransUnion and Equifax. Experian, the largest with over 100 million credit files on both individuals and businesses, processes millions of credit reports annually and discloses this information to millions of business subscribers – such as the banks, lenders and nearly every other business that extends credit. Subscribers pay these credit bureaus a fee to obtain your credit profile, and apparently each subscriber considers their ability to check your credit a good investment. Subscribers view your credit history as the best indicator of your creditworthiness. How promptly you paid past creditors reflects how likely you are to pay future creditors. Subscribers also check credit files to verify information on credit applications.

Subscribers who receive credit information from you may also exchange this new credit information with the credit bureaus. Whenever you apply for credit, your information may be forwarded to one or more credit bureaus. It is this constant updating between subscribers and the credit bureaus that keep your credit information current.

Collectively, the three national credit reporting bureaus maintain credit files on over 200 million Americans and over 12 million businesses. But each of the three credit bureaus can track the credit history of any American, regardless of where he or she may relocate. Each credit bureau is also likely to have a credit report on you, although their credit information will not necessarily be the same. Information that appears on one credit report may not be on another. That is why a more diligent creditor will check the credit reports from all three credit bureaus for a fuller picture of your credit history.

Subscribers who most commonly receive and issue credit information include the commercial banks, (including their credit card departments), other credit card companies, larger savings and loans, major department stores and finance companies. Yet, not every subscriber reports credit data to the credit bureaus, and some subscribers do not report their entire credit file. The less-frequently reporting subscribers are the utilities, hospitals, credit unions, merchant and oil company credit cards, and bank checking and savings departments. It is for this reason that a bounced check probably will not appear on your credit report. Credit bureaus and their subscribers transfer this account information electronically.

How do the credit reporting agencies operate?

Whenever you apply for credit, your prospective creditor will ask a local credit agency for your credit report or/and FICO® score. To activate this request, the creditor enters your name and social security number electronically to the agency. In moments, your creditor receives your complete credit profile directly from the local credit agency. Your local credit agency, in turn, obtains your credit file from one or more of the three national bureaus with whom it is affiliated. However, it is only the three national bureaus that compile and disseminate credit information. The local credit agencies are essentially middlemen whose function is to disseminate this information to their local subscribers.

Prospective creditors can obtain credit information directly from the three national bureaus, and they often do. Whether a prospective creditor obtains credit information about you directly – or through a local credit agency – what is important is that the three national bureaus report the best possible credit profile about you.

Who are the three major credit bureaus and how do I contact them?

The three major credit bureaus (or what the Fair Credit Reporting Act defines as 'consumer reporting agencies') are:

- Experian Credit Information Service (formerly TRW)
  P.O. Box 2104
  Allen, TX 75013-2004
  www.experian.com
  Tel. 888-397-3742

- TransUnion LLC
  Consumer Disclosure Center
  P.O. Box 2000
  Chester, PA 19022-2000
  www.tuc.com
  Tel. 800-916-8800

- EQUIFAX Credit Information Services
  P.O. Box 740241
  Atlanta, GA 30374-0241
  www.equifax.com
  Tel. 888-766-0008

How do the credit bureaus get all this credit information about me?

Before the computer era, it was, of course, more difficult for the credit bureaus to compile full credit histories. Now it is easily accomplished through vast computer networks that instantly transmit and compile credit information about you from three primary sources: 1) information you provide; 2) your creditors; 3) public records.

Not surprisingly, you provide a great deal of personal information whenever you apply for credit. For instance, you may divulge your social security number, job, salary, current and previous address, bank accounts, credit cards and other credit references. A more extensive credit application will also have you disclose your assets, liabilities, alimony payments, lawsuits, judgments and prior bankruptcies, as well as considerable other information. Because you voluntarily provide so much credit information about yourself, you can see why it is so important to accurately complete your credit applications, and provide favorable information, while at the same time avoiding unnecessary disclosures that can only harm your credit.

Your former and current creditors also furnish information about you to the credit bureaus. They particularly disclose whether you punctually pay your obligations. Creditors who provide this credit information may do so as either automatic or limited subscribers.

Automatic subscribers routinely supply credit information to the credit bureaus, usually monthly. Automatic subscribers report the date they first extended you credit, your largest credit balance, repayment terms, whether you pay punctually or whether it was necessary to pursue collection or 'charge-off' your account. Banks, credit unions, finance companies, larger merchants, collection agencies and the major credit card companies (American Express, MasterCard, Visa, and Discover) are automatic subscribers. Smaller and less-frequent users of credit information are usually limited subscribers.

Limited subscribers usually do not exchange information with the credit bureaus; they only 'buy' credit information. Nevertheless, a limited subscriber may report to the credit bureau an outstanding or overdue obligation. Therefore, a limited subscriber will probably not help your credit rating when you pay punctually, but they can badly damage your credit if you do not.

Finally, considerable credit-related information is compiled from the public records which disclose lawsuits, judgments, bankruptcies, divorces, foreclosures, tax liens, wage garnishments and criminal convictions. There are a number of private firms that search the public records for this information, which they then sell to the credit bureaus.

What are the most common reasons for credit denial?

There are endless possibilities for credit declination, but here are the six most common reasons according to the credit bureaus:

1. Delinquent credit obligations: Late payments, bad debts, or legal judgments against you obviously make you a higher risk credit customer, and lower your chances for credit.

2. Incomplete credit application: If you omit important information on your credit application or make other errors on your application, there may be a significant discrepancy between your application and your credit file, which can hurt your chances for credit. Creditors want a consistency of information.

3. Excessive 'inquiries': Every creditor inquiry is noted on your credit record. Inquiries happen whenever you apply for credit and the prospective creditor requests information about you from the credit bureau, and when you request your own credit report, it also generates an inquiry, but it is not an adverse entry on your record. As few as four credit inquiries within a six month period may be viewed as excessive credit activity, and prospective creditors may then presume that you are trying unsuccessfully to find credit elsewhere.

4. Errors in your file: Errors arise. Unfortunately, even simple clerical mistakes (confusing your name with someone with a similar name or recent address change, etc.) can create credit problems. Because credit bureaus handle millions of files, there is always that possibility of error. Your goal is to find and correct these errors, which means that you must periodically and carefully review your credit file for accuracy, and then take whatever steps are necessary to correct those errors.

5. Insufficient credit history: Your 'credit history' may also be too scanty for the type or amount of credit you request. You must then further build your credit to qualify for the credit-line you require.

6. Tax liens, bankruptcy, judgments, foreclosures or repossessions are all 'red flags' that automatically damage credit, and sometimes eliminate the possibility of obtaining any significant credit.

Who can obtain copies of my credit report?

Not everyone has the right to get your credit report. The Fair Credit Reporting Act (FCRA) allows only businesses and individuals with a legitimate business need for your credit information in connection with a business transaction that involves you, to access your credit information. This authorization, however, goes beyond prospective creditors to whom you apply for credit – such as credit card issuers and lenders. There are others who can check your credit report:

- Insurance companies (they may want credit information to decide whether to sell you insurance or change your premiums).

- Employers (who have your permission, and who may want credit information to determine whether to hire or promote you).

- Any business or individual who has your written authorization to check your credit.

- The Federal Government, if they consider you are a security risk.

- The IRS (with a subpoena).

- State and local child support enforcement agencies.

- Anyone with a court order that authorizes them access to your credit information.

- Anyone with a valid business reason to review your credit file concerning a business transaction that you initiated.

Of course, you always have the absolute right to review your own credit information.

Any authorized parties may review your credit file only for a credit-related purpose. It violates federal law for someone without a legitimate credit-related purpose to request your credit file.

Can I 'block' someone from accessing my credit report if they otherwise have the right to access my credit file under the FCRA.

No. Credit files are considered public record to those who have the statutory right to access this information.

Why would an employer want a credit check on an employee?

Employers oftentimes do credit checks to evaluate an employees (or prospective employees) ability to handle their own finances. A credit history can also indicate the risk of theft or bribery, particularly if the employee has excess debt. Good credit is also a sign of stability, and a good credit rating may be necessary for an employee to be bonded.

Under federal law, an employee must give an employer or prospective employer written consent for a credit check, but once this consent is granted, the employer can continuously receive future credit reports without further written authorization.

Why would good credit be important to an insurance company?

Most life and health insurers routinely obtain a prospective insured's credit report before they issue a policy. They check medical information from the Medical Information Bureau (MIB) in Boston, but they also check credit records to verify other information on an application, determine the applicant's financial stability and evaluate whether the insurance prospect is likely to pay the insurance premiums.

Does every business report account information to the national credit bureaus?

Most businesses transmit information only when an account is delinquent or the creditor has sued to collect. These creditors include utilities, smaller retailers, professionals (lawyers and physicians), insurance companies and landlords. Banks and credit card issuers usually report both good and bad credit experiences.

TWO

HOW GOOD IS YOUR CREDIT?

How do you improve your credit? It starts by obtaining a copy of your credit report and FICO® score from each of the three national credit bureaus. Once you have these reports, you must carefully review them for mistakes and any other negative information that may, for one reason or another, be incorrect and thus subject to correction or deletion.

Credit repair is not a 'one-time' process. Even when you have an error-free credit report, you must continuously review your report to keep it as accurate and positive as possible.

There is no great mystery to understanding your credit report. I will explain the process in this chapter. You will also find more information about credit reports from each of the three national credit bureaus. Once you understand the process to review and interpret your credit report, you can thereafter quickly monitor your credit history with minimum time and effort.

How do I get a copy of my credit report?

One fast way is to go to *www.annualcreditreport.com* or phone 1-877-322-8228. Or write directly to the credit bureaus. (See sample letters.) Your letter should include: 1) your full name (and any aliases or maiden name); 2) current address; 3) former address; 4) social security number; 5) spouse's name (voluntary); and 6) whether you have been denied credit within 30 days (include a copy of the credit denial or the details).

The credit bureaus may ask you for additional information (such as a photocopy of your driver's license). If you personally visit the credit bureau, the bureau will have you complete their own credit report request form that asks for essentially the same information.

Another easy way to get your credit report is to contact the three credit bureaus online:

- Experian Credit Information Service (formerly TRW)
  www.experian.com
- TransUnion LLC
  www.transunion.com
- EQUIFAX Credit Information Services
  www.equifax.com

Will the credit bureaus charge me a fee for my credit report?

As of September, 2005; credit reports are issued once annually free of charge. The credit bureaus may charge a fee of $7 to $10 for more frequent reports, or they may charge extra for your FICO® score.

Are the three national credit bureaus the only sources of credit information?

No. There are many other sources. For instance, U.D. Registry specializes in providing landlords with information on evictions, and other firms report only 'bounced' check histories, ATM usage or debit card information. Also, certain industries chiefly rely upon their own industry credit reporting network.

Should I order my credit report from all three credit bureaus, or would one report be sufficient to check my credit?

Review your credit report from each of the three bureaus. Keep in mind that credit bureaus compile their information from their subscribers and since they do not necessarily share the same subscribers, they will probably have different credit information on you. Each bureau may also have different errors and omissions on their reports.

What information will be on my credit report?

Credit reports vary somewhat in format, but always include:

1. *Identification information:* your full name, last two addresses, social security number, date of birth, and place of employment. Length of employment and income are not usually reported (and when it is reported, is often incorrect). Creditors frequently reject credit applications when they cannot confirm employment. For example, if you are self-employed, the credit bureau may incorrectly list you as unemployed – which you should correct immediately.

2. *Detailed information about each listed account:* Name of the issuer, the date the account was opened, original balance or limit, current balance (beginning with the reporting date, which is also listed), terms of account and the current status of the account. The status of each item follows a coding system that details the account history. This is why you cannot pay a delinquent account and change your status to 'cleared.' An example is CO NOW PAY which means that the account was a 'charge-off,' by the creditor but that you are now paying on the account.

3. *Public record information:* Bankruptcies, tax liens, judgments, lawsuits, foreclosures, divorces and other public filings.

4. *Credit report requests*: whenever someone requests a copy of your report it is recorded in your report and remains on your record for up to one year. This addition is 'non-evaluated' by the bureau, but it can become a 'negative' if you have too many inquiries within a certain time period, with comparatively few opened accounts. Prospective creditors may then question why you were turned down, though there are many possible reasons for credit inquiries.

5. *Consumer statement:* Finally, your report will include a space for you to insert a consumer statement which may challenge or explain any creditor entry in your file (up to 100 words).

What information cannot legally be included on my credit report?

Your credit report cannot contain information concerning your race, religion, sex, national origin or personal lifestyle, nor can you be denied credit due to any of these factors. Your credit report also cannot contain information concerning your character.

Some credit applications request the names and addresses of relatives or associates. Can they be contacted for credit information about me?

No. Credit applications can request the names and addresses of relatives or associates, however, the credit bureaus cannot contact them for credit information. They may be contacted only to verify your residence, employment or to locate you should you default on payment to a creditor.

How does an Investigative Consumer Report differ from a credit report?

Do not confuse a credit report with an Investigative Consumer Report which is not used for credit purposes. Investigative Consumer Reports are prepared by companies which specialize in compiling detailed profiles on individuals. Investigative Consumer Reports contain considerably more personal information than do credit reports. However, the Federal Fair Credit Reporting Act requires that you be notified if an Investigative Consumer Report on you is requested.

Will my credit report reflect my entire credit history? I noticed that many of my accounts are not listed on my credit record.

Your credit report probably will not reflect your entire credit history. Many creditors are limited subscribers to the credit bureaus,

> Your credit report will not reflect your entire credit history. What is important is that those relatively few reports transactions that do appear, be both accurate and favorable.

and they will not release or exchange your credit information to the credit bureaus. Other creditors may be unaffiliated with a credit bureau which is why only a comparatively small percentage of your actual credit transactions will appear on your credit report. What is important is that those relatively few reported transactions that do appear, be both accurate and favorable.

When I received my credit report, I also received a confirmation number. What is its purpose?

The confirmation number is essentially a tracking number that allows you to conveniently follow up on credit inquiries by fax, phone or e-mail.

How do I read my credit report?

Once you have your credit report, you must identify every potential credit problem. Locate and circle every negative mark or 'ding' on your credit report. Information on your credit report is coded much like the coding on your bank statements. To help you understand your credit report, the FCRA requires that the credit bureau explain any entry on their report that you would not otherwise reasonably understand. Look for their coding symbols. Next, hunt those damaging remarks within the four sections of your credit report:

1. *The Historical Status records of your monthly payments.* This will ideally be free of 'past due' marks which reflect 30, 60 or 90-day 'overdues.' Many 'past due' marks are entered accidentally, or because a payment was received late, or because of delay in processing your payment. (Of course, you may have actually paid late.) To avoid late payment marks, your payments must be credited to your account by the due date, not merely mailed by the due date.

2. *The Comments section* may contain a wide variety of remarks as 'charged to P&L.' ('P&L' means 'profit and loss.') When a creditor charges an account to profit and loss, it is charged off as a bad debt and the creditor no longer anticipates payment. There are other negative entries to watch for:

> *Coll Acct.* – Your account has been assigned to a collection agency because it was seriously past due.

> *Curr Was For.* – Foreclosure proceedings were started on your account, but you repaid all past due amounts and the account is now current.

> *Curr Was 30-2.* – Twice your account has been 30 days past due, but is now current.

> *Deed In Lieu.* – In order to avoid foreclosure, you gave your creditor a deed to your property.

> *Del Was 120.* – Your account was 120 days past due. Although you since made some payments, your account remains 30, 60 or 90 days late.

> *Govclaim.* – The government filed a claim against you because you defaulted on a government loan.

> *Foreclosure.* – Your creditor foreclosed on your property.

> *Not Pay AA.* – You have an outstanding balance, but are not paying according to a negotiated agreement to repay.

> *Repo.* – Your creditor repossessed your property because you failed to repay a loan.

Vol Surr. – You voluntarily surrendered your property to prevent repossession by a creditor.

30 Day Del. – You are at least 30 days late on one or more payments on your account.

Any of these or similar marks, of course, will damage your credit.

3. *Inquiries from prospective creditors* are also listed in the report. Excessive credit inquiries may be viewed by a potential creditor as a sign of financial difficulty and that you are seeking more credit as a solution. Creditors often refuse credit because of 'too many' inquiries. However, certain inquiries are not reported to prospective creditors. These include your own requests to review your credit report, credit reports requested for promotional purposes, and requests from current creditors who may want to review or update your file.

4. *Public record data* appear in your credit report. Also examine these entries closely for accuracy.

   ▪ Bankruptcy – bankruptcy admits that you once were financially unable to pay your debts when due.

   ▪ Tax Lien – an IRS or state tax lien was entered against your property because you owe back taxes.

   ▪ Judgment – you lost a lawsuit, either at trial or because you failed to defend, and there is now an outstanding judgment on record against you.

   ▪ Settled – you resolved a pending lawsuit before trial.

- Child Support – you failed to pay court-ordered child support.

- Withdrawn – your bankruptcy case was with-drawn.

- Dismissed – a lawsuit against you was dismissed because either the court ruled in your favor or the creditor failed to pursue its claim.

- Discharged – you filed bankruptcy and the court relieved you of your debts.

- Paid and Satisfied – you fully paid a court judgment or an account turned over for collection to a collection agency or attorney.

- Suit – a legal action remains pending against you.

5. *Account Profile column* contains a summary rating for each account. A summary may read 'positive,' 'negative' or 'non-rated.' 'Positive' means you pay on time. 'Negative' indicates that you have a serious credit problem, such as a defaulted debt. 'Non-rated' may signify a few late payments among many more prompt payments. (This can still hurt your credit, even when there is no one strong negative entry.) Every negative or non-rated entry has a code that reflects the specific problem. Your goal: Remove every negative or non-rated mark on your credit report.

6. *Personal information* is another potentially troublesome section which must be checked carefully. Bureaus employ 'alert codes' to highlight conflicting information in your file. The entry of such terms as 'HAWK ALERT, TransAlert, AKA search, or CHECKPOINT' on your credit report

indicates that you may have attempted to alter your file, though conflicting information sometimes results instead from clerical error. For instance, one incorrect digit in your social security number may make it appear that you are attempting to defraud creditors. Or the alert can mean that the credit bureau received four or more inquiries about your report within the prior 60 days. The credit bureau is then warning prospective creditors that you may have a sudden need for credit. Or the alert may indicate that the credit bureau believes that your residential address is a commercial address. Alert signals indicate a possible attempt by the credit consumer to deceive the credit bureau and its subscribers.

Finally, the credit bureaus now use an index or 'delinquency indicator' to more accurately predict whether you will promptly pay your debts. Credit bureaus are not required to disclose the measurements they use in their index nor explain how to read it. Consequently, you cannot dispute the accuracy of an indexed credit score.

> Credit bureaus are not required to disclose the measurements they use in their index nor explain how to read it.

Do all credit reports disclose information in the same manner?

No. Equifax, TransUnion and Experian each follow different formats, and while their reports all contain similar information, their precise reporting format varies. That is why it is important to review your credit reports individually.

Can you explain in more detail what other entries and notations I may find under the account file?

A number of other possible entries may be included under 'account information,' (the specific entries will depend upon the credit bureau). A typical listing will include:

▪ *Company name* – the company reporting the credit information.

▪ *Type account* – whether it is a credit card, line of credit, loan, student loan, etc.

▪ *Current status* – i.e. charge-off, collection account closed by consumer, account closed by creditor, etc.

▪ *Account number* – the account number, if one was assigned by the creditor.

▪ *Account responsibility* – who is responsible for the account. This may be coded as:

> I = individual
> J = joint
> C = co-maker
> B = on behalf of another
> A = authorized on a third
> S = shared
> T = terminated
> U = undesignated

▪ *Date opened* – month and year the account was opened.

▪ *Date of last activity* – the last date activity was reported on this account. (This may be a payment date or disposition of account – collection, charge-off, etc.)

- *Type account* – this also may be coded, such as:
  - I = installment (monthly payment)
  - O = open (payable in full/month)
  - R = revolving (payments vary)

- *High credit* – maximum credit line or balance outstanding.

- *Terms* – number of monthly payments remaining to fully pay the debt.

- *Balance* – present outstanding balance (when last reported).

- *Past due* – amount past due as last reported.

- *Date reported* – when the creditor provided the information.

How do I check the inquiries on my credit report?

The three credit bureaus distinguish between the different types of inquiries, as well as which are disclosed to prospective creditors. For instance, TransUnion divides inquiries (those who requested a copy of your report) into sections. The first section is 'Regular Inquiries' from creditors who requested your full credit report. The second section are 'Promotional Inquiries' from those who want to offer you credit (credit cards, insurance, etc.). The third section 'Account Review Inquiries,' identifies those creditors who wanted to inspect a specific account. Promotional Inquiries and Account Review Inquiries are not disclosed to other creditors. On the other hand, Equifax's coding system identifies the type inquiry.

How long do inquiries remain on my credit report?

It depends on the type inquiry and the credit bureau. For example, Equifax retains most inquiries for two years.

How does a creditor quickly evaluate my overall credit status?

While a prospective (or present) creditor will probably carefully review your overall credit report, it is now more common for a creditor to simply check your credit score – a numerical summation of your creditworthiness as established by a commercial credit scoring service.

Who determines my credit score?

Fair Isaac, Inc. is the principal provider of credit scores. Their score is referred to as the FICO® score. FICO®, in fact, has become synonymous with credit scores. While Fair Isaac designed the credit scoring system for each of the three national credit bureaus, each bureau generates their own scores under different names. Experian's is the Experian/Fair Isaac Risk Score; TransUnion calls its score EMPIRICA; and Equifax, BEACON.

How is my FICO® score determined?

Your FICO® score is a numerical evaluation of your present creditworthiness. The credit score is compiled directly from both the positive and negative entries in your credit report. The score is divided into five categories, allocated as follows:

1.   Type of credit you use = 10 percent

2.   Your credit history = 35 percent

3. Amount you currently owe = 30 percent

4. Length of your credit history = 15 percent

5. New credit obtained = 10 percent

Equifax's scoring system ranges between 300 and 850 points; TransUnion's between 150 and 934; Experian's 340 to 820.

For example, under Experian's Beacon scoring system, a FICO® score of:

340-600 = highest risk to the lender (lowest score)

601-660 = medium-high risk

661-720 = medium risk

721-780 = medium-low risk

781-850 = lowest risk (highest score)

Together with your numerical FICO® credit score, you will also receive a national percentile ranking which reflects the percentage of the US population with credit scores higher or lower than yours. For example, an Experian credit score of 800 places you into the 92 percentile. Eight percent of the population has higher scores, and 92 percent are lower.

A higher score, of course, indicates a lower potential delinquency rate – or the rate at which 100 borrowers in a specific range will default on a loan, declare bankruptcy or fall 90 or more days behind in payment. Thus, a delinquency rate of 50 percent means that for every 100 borrowers, 50 will represent one or more credit problems.

What minimum FICO® score should I aim for?

Credit experts agree that a 720 FICO® score is necessary to be considered a good credit risk. A

Credit experts agree that a 720 FICO® score is necessary to be considered a good credit risk.

lower score may cause you either to be denied credit, or your credit will be on less favorable terms. If you follow the recommendations in this book, you should increase your score at least by 50-100 points.

I have three different FICO® scores: TransUnion 670, Experian 720 and Equifax 740. Why do I have different scores, and how do prospective creditors decide which score to use?

Most creditors look at your middle score. In this case, it would be Experian's 720. For this reason, it is sometimes wise to try to raise your middle score before you work on the credit reports with the lower and higher score.

Is it possible to change my FICO® score in as little as one day?

Yes, but you must do it on-line and follow a three step process.

1. Submit an immediate protest to any credit mark you want to dispute.

2. Simultaneously, notify your creditor of the dispute and request that they temporarily suspend the negative entry pending the investigation. Larger creditors, such as MB-NAVisa will do this as a matter of policy.

3. Fax any proof of deletions (or temporary suspensions), and request that they immediately change your report.

Will my FICO® score come with my credit report?

Not necessarily. Some credit bureaus charge extra for their FICO® score.

What is the easiest way to find out my FICO® score?

To get your FICO® score from Fair Isaac, go to *www.myfico.com*. Or go to the websites of the three national credit bureaus. Or, request it by phone and mail. You can also log onto *www.freecreditreport.com* and specifically request your FICO® score.

Will every prospective creditor rely on my FICO® scores to evaluate my credit?

No. Nor is a FICO® score the only credit measure. There are others, and many lenders rely upon their own internal credit-scoring system though most lenders do rely heavily on FICO® scores, at least to initially evaluate your credit.

Lenders chiefly use a supplemental scoring system to establish how much credit they will extend to you. While a loan officer or credit manager may deny you credit unless you have a minimum FICO® score (the score required is predetermined by the creditor's policy-making committee), the loan officer or credit manager may use FICO® only as a guide to determine whether to further consider your loan or credit request. Most lending institutions utilize both FICO® and their own standardized scoring systems to make more objective loan decisions. For instance, banks know from experience, that if you have a certain salary, say

$50,000, you can, perhaps, only comfortably handle a combined maximum credit card line (i.e. $5,000). Or a lender may consider people who move frequently, have no telephone, or a poor job history as poor credit risks. Scoring tests reveal these patterns. While the loan officer's personal judgment about the borrower is always important, banks rely less on a loan officer's subjective evaluation of the borrower. By combining FICO® scores with objective standards set by their own scoring system, they incur fewer 'bad' loans.

While the loan officer's personal judgment about the borrower is always important, banks rely less on a loan officer's subjective evaluation of the borrower. By combining FICO® scores with objective standards set by their own scoring system, they incur fewer 'bad' loans.

What impact may it have on my FICO® score if I can get a negative mark deleted?

The removal of even one negative entry can improve your FICO® score by 25 points or more! So, if you can delete four negative entries, you may add 100 points to your score. And that will have considerable impact on your credit.

What other credit factors may a lender consider?

While each lender sets its own credit-scoring system; there are common considerations. Once you know what specific credit criteria a lender uses, you can identify and focus on those specific entries on your credit profile which will improve your credit score. An example of a 'Credit Scoring System' asks (with corresponding points):

1. Years at present job?

        Less than one year   0

        One to two years   1

Two to four years	2
Four to ten years	3
Over ten years	4

2. Monthly income level?

Less than $1,000	0
$2,000 to $2,500	1
$2,500 to $5,000	2
Over $5,000	3

3. Present obligations past due?

Yes	0
No	1

4. Total monthly debt payments compared to income after taxes?

50 percent	0
40 to 49 percent	1
30 to 39 percent	2
under 30 percent	3

5. Prior loans with lender?

No	0
Yes, but not closed	0
Yes, but closed with two or less 11-day notices	1

6. Checking account?

None	0
Yes	1
Yes	2

7. Length at present address?
    Less than three years   0
    Three years or more   1

8. Age of newest automobile?
    Over one year old   0
    Less than one year old   1

9. Savings account with lender?
    No   0
    Yes   1

10. Own real estate?
    No   0
    Yes   3

11. Telephone in your own name?
    No   0
    Yes   1

12. Good credit references?
    No   0
    Yes   1

You will find similar questions on most credit scoring applications. The specific questions asked and their respective points are set by each lender's Consumer Credit Policy Committee, who also prepares guidelines to apply the scoring system as a guide to the loan officer. Nevertheless, scoring systems can vary considerably between lenders, and sometimes even within the same organization. For example, when loan funds are plentiful, the lending standards are less strictly enforced than when money is tight.

How good is your score? Here's how a loan officer may evaluate it (based on possible points):

- 0 to 50 percent (of possible points): Reject outright. Don't waste time on this application.

- 50 to 60 percent: Review carefully. Do not ap-prove unless there are other good reasons to grant credit.

- 60 to 70 percent: Review with a bias toward approval. (This profiles the typical credit consumer and indicates a reasonable risk.)

- 70 to 90 percent: Grant the loan unless there is good reason to deny.

- 90 to 100 percent: Automatically grant credit within reasonable limits.

If you fall under 50 percent and your application is rejected, don't give up. You may possibly secure a smaller loan, pledge collateral or find a cosigner. (A cosigner's credit guarantees your obligations to get your loan approved.) As an example, if you are an unemployed student who needs a car loan, and your parents co-sign; it is your parent's' credit that would be evaluated.

If your credit score falls between 40 to 90 percent, you will get a closer credit review. If you are above 90 percent then you can generally get a reasonable amount of unsecured credit only on your signature.

What factors can lower my credit scores?

Many factors lower a FICO® score (which gives you as many opportunities to improve your score, as I will later show you). However, here are the most common reasons for a low FICO® score:

1. Excessive delinquent accounts, ('slow pay' or 'no pay' or accounts turned over for collection or 'charged off.' (The creditor has stopped pursuing collection and does not expect payment).

2. Outstanding judgments, tax liens, foreclosures, repossessions or bankruptcy.

3. An excess number of outstanding credit cards (which increases the likelihood of excessive debt).

4. Too many current accounts with high balances (regardless of your ability to pay, lenders see this as a potential problem).

5. Failure to significantly reduce loan balances (your debt level is too high in relation to your total credit limit or your original loan balance).

These are the most common 'credit killers' to watch for on your credit report, and you must have deleted them if you are to have good credit.

A lenders' evaluation of your credit history and FICO® score are but two significant factors in the credit decision. Income, employment history, assets, liabilities and other considerations also significantly influence the credit decision. While there are many different scoring models (not every bureau uses the same model), every lender uses a scoring method to summarize and quantify your creditworthiness.

Doesn't the credit bureau automatically check the accuracy of my credit report?

No. Credit bureaus accept any negative information about you at face value. The credit bureaus have no obligation to check the accuracy of your credit information until you challenge it. Unfortunately, prospective creditors oftentimes rely upon misinformation, and because the credit bureau has no responsibility to check accuracy, it is you who must keep your credit report accurate.

THREE ■ ■ ■

HOW TO REPAIR BAD CREDIT

To repair your credit, you must assert your legal rights as a credit consumer. But before you can assert your legal rights to improve your credit score, you must know your legal rights. For this we turn to the Fair Credit Reporting Act (FCRA). The FCRA is primarily concerned with the regulation of credit bureaus and credit reports. The FCRA has two purposes: 1) To protect you against credit abuse, and 2) to provide you the legal tools necessary to repair and improve your credit.

What are your rights if your credit report contains false, misleading or incomplete information which damages your credit? Turn to the Fair Credit Reporting Act (FCRA), which protects you against credit abuse and an unfair credit profile. The FCRA gives you several important rights as a credit consumer. You must take advantage of these important rights; they are the keys to erasing those negative marks on your credit report.

When can I challenge the accuracy of my credit report?

You have the right to challenge the accuracy of your credit report at any time. Your right to challenge your report is contained in the FCRA's 'Procedure in case of disputed accuracy.' 'Disputed accuracy' refers to any information

> You have the right to challenge the accuracy of your credit report at any time.

in your credit report that is false, obsolete, incomplete or incorrectly entered, in whole or in part.

What are the most common errors to look for on my credit report?

Correct any information which is inaccurate, incomplete or not allowed by law to remain on your credit file. Specifically, look for:

▪ incorrect or incomplete name, address, phone number, social security number or birthdate;

▪ incorrect marital status;

▪ incorrect or missing employment information;

▪ commingled accounts (credit histories belonging to someone with a similar or same name);

▪ lawsuits and judgments older than seven years;

▪ bankruptcies older than ten years (or that does not specify whether it is a Chapter 7, 11 or 13);

▪ duplicate accounts (i.e. the same account information appearing twice);

▪ debts of a spouse;

▪ paid or discharged tax liens, judgments or mechanics lien;

▪ foreclosures or repossessions that did not occur;

▪ accounts that you closed and were not marked 'closed by consumer';

▪ incorrect account information.

For how long can negative information remain on my credit record?

The FCRA sets the time period negative information can remain on your credit report. Stale information is obsolete and must be removed. For example, the law allows a bankruptcy filing or an unpaid IRS tax lien to remain on your credit report for 10 years. A Chapter 13 can stay on your credit record for only 7 years. Other negative credit information becomes obsolete after 7 years and must, at your request, then be removed.

I'm applying for a home mortgage and I have two negative marks on my credit report that are hurting my credit score. Solutions?

If the items are accurate, the creditor may agree to temporarily delete (up to six months) the negative mark if you explain that you are making a major purchase.

> If the items are accurate, the creditor may agree to temporarily delete (up to six months) the negative mark if you explain that you ar making a major purchase.

Some will do it as a matter of good will, and others because they may fear a lawsuit or want to otherwise avoid the hassle of defending the entry.

I sold my home nearly a year ago and paid off the mortgage, but TransUnion still shows the mortgage balance on my credit report. How can I get it removed?

The fastest way is to get a payoff letter from the bank and fax it to TransUnion.

How do I dispute a negative entry on my credit report?

You can dispute any negative credit entry, and when you do, you neither admit nor deny your liability for the debt. You are only challenging the accuracy of the entry or mark reported on your credit report.

It is important to understand that the credit bureau must 'reinvestigate' any negative entry that you challenge. The FCRA requires that the credit bureau then contact the creditor and request that the creditor verify whatever negative information you dispute that appears on your credit report. Remember, anyone – whether or not a legitimate creditor – can enter negative information on your credit report with neither your consent nor knowledge, and without the need to first prove that the information is true. The credit bureaus only report this information, they do not investigate the information's accuracy – until and unless *you* challenge it!

> It is important to understand that the credit bureau must 'reinvestigate' any negitive entry that you challenge.

What must the credit bureau do once I challenge a negative credit entry?

The credit bureau must investigate within 30 days (or a reasonable time period thereafter) any item that you dispute on your report. One exception is that the credit bureau has a 15 day extension if the credit consumer offers additional information about the disputed item. The credit bureau must then notify the creditor to confirm and verify the accuracy of their negative information.

This process shifts the burden of proof back on the creditor. And compliance can be burdensome for the creditor.

For example, a creditor may need to verify information that is no longer available or convenient to recover (i.e. the creditor must locate and search old files). Remember, the creditor must thoroughly check his information for accuracy and completeness. The creditor must also respond to the credit bureau within 30 days of notice of your protest and present convincing proof of its claim or the entry reported against you. This is too burdensome a task for many creditors to comply with within the required time, and for this reason many negative marks are automatically deleted only because the creditor defaulted in defending their negative entry against the credit consumer's challenge.

> The creditor must also respond to the credit bureau within 30 days of the notice of your protest and present convincing proof of its claim or entry reported against you.

What do I do if the creditor cannot or does not verify the accuracy of their information to the credit bureau within 30 days?

Upon your demand, the credit bureau must then delete the negative entry from your credit report. This is their obligation under the FCRA.

How often do negative items get deleted because the creditor didn't respond to the dispute?

The odds are about 40 percent that a creditor will not defend a disputed entry, and this is true even when their entry is accurate.

What if a credit bureau violates the FCRA and refuses to delete information they are required to remove. Can I sue them?

The FCRA gives consumers the rights to sue credit bureaus for negligence or willful non-compliance with the law.

Yes. The FCRA gives consumers the right to sue credit bureaus for negligence or willful non-compliance with the law. The lawsuit must be commenced within two years after the date of the bureau's harmful behavior. You can sue for actual damages, punitive damages (when the wrongful act was malicious or willful), attorneys' fees, costs and interest.

Can I sue a creditor who wrongfully refuses to delete an incorrect credit mark?

If you believe the creditor has violated your rights under FCRA, you can sue and ask a judge t issue an injunction compelling the creditor to remove the negitive mark.

If you believe the creditor has violated your rights under the FCRA, you can sue and ask a judge to issue an injunction compelling the creditor to remove the negative mark. You can also sue for any monetary damage that you sustain. However, an attorney's letter to a recalcitrant creditor may convince the creditor to cooperate, and there are lawyers who specialize in consumer credit law.

What happens if the creditor verifies the accuracy of the negative credit information?

If the creditor verifies the accuracy of the information within the 30 days, the negative mark will remain on your record. But if you still dispute the information you can submit a Consumer Statement explaining your view of the problem. In other words, as a credit consumer, you can dispute the accuracy of information on your report, and if you receive no satisfaction from the bureau or the creditor, then the credit bureau must attach your explanation (not to exceed 100 words) to every copy of your credit report that it later submits on inquiries.

Can I directly challenge a negative mark with a creditor?

Absolutely. The FCRA allows you to directly challenge creditors who claim you paid late, defaulted, etc. Send them a letter demanding proof of their claim and demand that they remove the negative item on your credit report within 10 days. If they don't provide proof, follow up with a second letter, demanding deletion. If they do not provide proof, send copies to the credit bureaus.

If a creditor defends against a protest once, wouldn't the creditor eventually give in if I sent repeated protests?

Some do. I have seen credit consumers write their creditor essentially the same dispute letter on a weekly basis until the creditor finally relented and deleted the negative item. They also disputed the item monthly to the credit bureau. Credit repair professionals are persistent when challenging costly negative marks – and you should be too.

So, now that I understand this much about credit repair, what is my first step?

Once you know your legal rights, and have your credit report in hand, you are now ready to fix your credit.

First step: find and circle every negative mark or 'ding' on your credit report. If the information on your credit report is coded, the credit bureau will explain their credit reports coding key.

Look for any damaging credit remark within each section of your credit report. For example, the Historical Status section records your monthly payments, and will ideally be free of 'past due' marks (30, 60 or 90 day periods). Most negative marks are 'past dues.' If you find any, then list each 'past due' account on a separate sheet of paper. How many past dues are there? How late were these payments? What percentage of your total accounts are delinquent? You will later see how to contest these 'negatives.' You will find that some 'past dues' may have been entered accidentally or because your payment was received late or because of a delay in processing your payment.

Next, check the Comments section for such remarks such as 'Charged to P&L' ('profit and loss'). When a creditor charges an account to profit and loss, they have charged it off as a bad debt and the creditor no longer expects payment.

Then look for credit inquiries from banks, stores, credit card companies or others to whom you applied for credit. Excessive credit inquiries may indicate that you need more credit. To counteract the negative effect of excess inquiries, add a 100-word (or less) statement to your credit report explaining the reasons for your many credit inquiries.

Don't forget to review the public records information on your credit report. You will there find tax liens, foreclosures bankruptcies or court judgments. Are any of these entries inaccurate? Can they be deleted? How can they be most favorably explained on your 100-word statement?

> Don't forget to review the public records information on your credit report. You will there find tax liens, foreclosures bankruptcies or court judgements.

Finally, closely review the credit report's 'Account Profile' for a summary rating for each account. A summary may read 'positive,' 'negative' or 'non-rated.' 'Positive' indicates good credit – you pay on time. 'Negative' indicates credit problems, such as a defaulted major debt or bankruptcy. 'Non-rated' suggests several late payments, which damages your credit. Every negative or non-rated entry is coded to reflect the nature of the problem. Your objective is to protest and remove every negative or non-rated mark.

Under what circumstance can I contest a negative mark?

You have the right to protest every negative mark to the credit bureau where you disagree with the entry. The credit bureau need only verify those marks that you dispute as erroneous, misleading or inaccurate.

For example, a 'Charge-off' indicates that the creditor charged your account to 'profit and loss,' and the creditor considers your debt uncollectible. But you can protest this comment if you paid the debt, since it should not be reported as 'charged-off'. Or you may have several 'Past dues'. Perhaps your payments were delayed due to post office delays when you changed addresses. Or you may believe you have paid on time.

Or you may dispute owing the creditor the exact amount the creditor claimed as delinquent or 'charged off.' Or perhaps you have been billed for unsatisfactory goods or services, and the creditor may have failed to resolve the problem to your satisfaction. Or the creditor may have delayed in resolving the problem to justify your delayed payment. As you can see, there are many possible reasons to dispute a negative credit mark.

> Negative information which is factually correct but that arises from extenuating or mitigating circumstances is best handdled through your own 100-word statement which will be added to your credit report.

Of course, you should send a protest letter only if the entry is factually incorrect or misleading or the delay was due to circumstances beyond your control. Negative information which is factually correct but that arises from extenuating or mitigating circumstances is best handled through your own 100-word statement which will be added to your credit report.

How do I protest a negative mark on my credit report?

To write your protests, use the sample letters in the back of this book as your guide. Do not use the dispute forms supplied by the credit bureaus because their dispute forms are deliberately designed to limit you to specific reasons for your dispute. The law, however, only requires you to provide a general reason to dispute a negative mark.

And it is important to provide only general reasons for your dispute. Don't be too specific. For example, don't recite correct amounts or dates. For instance, if the credit bureau inaccurately reports that you owe a creditor $1,500 when you owe only $1,475; your protest should state only that you never owed that creditor $1,500. You need not say what amount you do owe, nor should you. Or your protest may simply claim that you never incurred that debt on that date. Say no more. Or if you paid the debt, say so, but do not disclose when you did pay or the credit bureau may add this as negative information to your report.

While the sample letters in this book can serve as a guide, vary them to your circumstances. Your letters should also not appear to have originated from a credit repair firm because such letters are oftentimes returned or ignored by the credit bureaus.

A handwritten letter gets more attention and starts the process sooner. Sign, date, and include your address, date of birth and social security number on every

> A handwritten letter gets more attention and starts the process sooner. Sign, date, and include your address, date of birth and social security number on every letter. Keep a copy for your records.

letter. Keep a copy for your records. Send each protest separately and on separate dates (certified mail, return, receipt) to prove the date the credit bureau received it, and include a copy of your credit report so the credit bureau checks the correct file.

Why can't I just phone the credit bureau to correct my credit information?

When you want to repair your credit, keep everything in writing! Do not communicate with a credit bureau by telephone or in person. Moreover, since your communications must contain certain information, (which is another reason to closely follow the format of the sample letters) you will also want to log each written communication to track when your correspondence was received by the credit bureau and when their reply is due.

How do I phone the national credit bureaus on consumer disputes if my written correspondence does not get results?

Call the credit bureau's toll-free number:

Experian	888-397-3742
Equifax	800-685-1111
TransUnion	800-916-8800

But do follow-up your phone calls with written confirmation.

What do I do once I send my protest to the credit bureau?

Wait for the credit bureau to reply. Under FCRA rules, the credit bureau must respond to your initial letter within 30 days. If the credit bureau does not reply within 30 days (or a reasonable time thereafter), then send a second letter demanding an immediate response to your protest. Sample letters are in the appendix for this purpose also.

Why do protests usually result in improved credit reports?

There are several reasons. One reason is that a creditor may agree with the correction. Once received, the credit bureau must notify the creditor of your dispute and request that the creditor 'verify' the negative credit entry. If the creditor agrees that you are correct and that the negative entry is due to their error, then the creditor should notify the credit bureau to clear your credit record.

More commonly, the creditor simply won't bother to verify the negative credit mark and then the creditor will not reply to the credit bureau. Since the negative credit mark against you remains unverified, the credit bureau must then remove the protested item from your credit report. This is how most negative credit marks are deleted from credit reports, so it's worth repeating the process:

1. Dispute the credit entry.

2. The credit bureau requests verification from the creditor.

3. The creditor (probably) fails to verify the adverse credit information.

4. The credit bureau must within 30 days report to you that since the disputed credit entry was unverified by the creditor, it will be deleted.

Won't the credit bureau verify the accuracy of negative credit information on their own?

No. The credit bureaus do not verify credit information. You must dispute any inaccurate entry and the bureau must then rely on the creditor to defend against your dispute. Only through proper creditor verification can a protested negative mark remain on your credit report.

Why do so few creditors defend against disputed, negative credit information?

The most common reason? Creditors are usually too busy. While creditors find it easy to report credit problems to a credit bureau, verification of the facts months or years later is usually far more troublesome. The creditor must locate your file, provide supporting documents, and furnish a detailed statement to defend their negative entry. Most creditors find it easier to then ignore verification requests which, of course, will clear your credit.

Isn't it unfair to take advantage of creditor apathy to clear a credit history?

No. Both the Federal Trade Commission and Congress believe that the burden should be on the creditor to defend whatever adverse credit marks they file against you. If the creditor cannot, or chooses not to defend against their negative credit entry, you as the credit consumer should not be penalized by their unverified credit mark!

What if the credit bureau verifies that the disputed mark is correct?

Many creditors do verify their negative entries. The credit bureau must then confirm this verification to you within the 30-day reply period. The credit bureau's notice to you will contain the creditor's statement and/or whatever documentation is provided by the creditor to verify their negative credit information. If they receive a well-documented reply from the creditor, the credit bureau probably will not delete the negative credit mark from your credit report.

I want to finance a car, but there is incorrect information on my credit report that's holding up the loan. How can I accelerate the verification process?

Tell the credit bureau that you are trying to get a car loan (or other financing) and request a 'rush' verification. The credit bureau may even delete the negative item on request without verification, or whenever verification of the negative mark is not cost-effective.

I am self-employed but my credit report lists me as unemployed. How can I correct this?

> If you write 'self-employed' on a credit application, a credit bureau may list you as unemployed.

If you write 'self-employed' on a credit application, a credit bureau may list you as unemployed. Notify the credit bureau to insert your correct employment status and in the future, list the name of a specific employer, even if you list your own name as the employer.

If a creditor does verify a negative entry, does this mean there is nothing further I can do to correct my credit report?

No. You still have options. For example, you can try to convince the credit bureau that you are correct. However, the credit bureau is not there to referee whether you or your creditor is correct on a disputed credit entry. The creditor need only provide the credit bureau reasonable evidence or information to verify or defend their negative credit entry against you. Once they do, the credit bureau can keep the negative mark on your record.

Though the credit bureau need not arbitrate disputes between you and your creditor, a credit bureau must act fairly and take reasonable care to make certain that it reports only truthful and accurate information. Therefore, the credit bureau must correct or delete information on your report to the extent that you can convince the credit bureau that a negative entry against you is erroneous, misleading – or even possibly so.

Build your case! Advise the credit bureau why the information is erroneous. Submit documents (cancelled checks, letters, etc.) which help prove your case.

Perhaps you have provided this detailed information when you first disputed your credit report. If the creditor defended the negative entry, your second letter may challenge specific points made by the creditor. However, a first protest letter should still only summarily challenge the negative mark with a brief explanation. Of course, if the creditor does not verify the reasons for the negative entry, the entry must be removed. Only when the creditor verifies your negative entry should you reply with a stronger case to convince the credit bureau that you – not your creditor – is correct.

If the credit bureau still refuses to change your credit report, another option is to talk directly to your creditor. Most creditors are reasonable and will listen and possibly agree that they made an error or in some other way unfairly penalized you with poor credit and will assent to the removal of the negative credit entry.

When should I add a brief statement to my credit file?

If you believe a credit bureau continues to improperly include information on your report, or you want to explain in the best light one or more negative items on your report, then you have the right under the FCRA to insert a brief statement in your report. A summary statement prepared with the assistance of a credit bureau is limited to one hundred words. Otherwise, there is no word limit. Nor must the credit bureau release your entire statement to a prospective creditor if you exceed 100 words. They have the right to instead furnish a summary of your statement. For this reason, your own statement should be clear, concise and under 100 words.

Can the credit bureau request additional information from me once I protest an entry?

Yes. Credit bureaus frequently do this through what is called a preliminary response. The credit bureau acknowledges receipt of your protest letter and advises you that the bureau has not concluded its investigation. Preliminary responses are used to request additional information. For example, it may be canceled checks or evidence that a tax lien or judgment was satisfied. Comply with these requests fully and quickly. When you reply, also ask the credit bureau when they can expect to complete their investigation and a final determination made on correcting your credit report.

I have sent several protest letters to one credit bureau who finally wrote me and asked me to prove my identity. Is this common?

Credit bureaus should verify identity. Your best response is to send them a copy of a bill from some creditor that reveals as little about you as possible. A current phone or utility bill, or similar account information, will ordinarily suffice. A copy of your driver's license, social security card or passport may also be provided.

One credit bureau refused to investigate my protest because they claimed that I was using a credit repair company to frivolously challenge my negative marks. How should I handle this?

If the credit bureau claims you are using a credit repair company and thus refuses to investigate, respond using sample letter #12 which is specifically designed to handle this problem. It is permissible for a credit repair firm to help you correct your credit.

I have sent several protests to a credit bureau and they replied that my protest was frivolous and that they will take no further action to investigate. Is this legal? What should I do?

It infrequently happens that a credit bureau may claim your dispute is 'frivolous or irrelevant' and ignore your request. Sample letter #11 is specifically for this situation. If the credit bureau fails to send you a final reply within 30 days (or such other reasonable time that they may

> It infrequently happens that credit bureau may claim your dispute is 'frivolous or irrelevant' and ignore your request.

specify), then the protested negative credit information against you must be removed. If the credit bureau refuses to correct your credit report, then threaten further action.

What should I do once I complete the credit repair process?

Request an updated credit report. Compare carefully your updated credit report against the original report. Mark every correction or deletion. Circle every negative entry that has advanced to a non-rated entry and every non-rated or negative entry that became a positive entry. You may not get the results you want on every protest on the first round, but with perseverance comes progress. However, you are likely to notice that the credit bureau has deleted some negative items only because those creditors did not respond to your protest. Try not to submit an updated credit report to a prospective creditor until you correct every possible negative entry on your credit report because you want a prospective creditor to see the best possible credit report.

What if I protested a negative entry and the credit bureau investigated and decided to keep the negative entry on my credit report based on the creditor's reply?

Wait a year or two and again challenge the negative entry. But raise a different dispute. If the creditor once verified a disputed entry, it would be frivolous to again dispute the same point. However, you can possibly raise a new dispute. And it may be worth the effort. Once again, the creditor may agree or fail to defend the negative entry.

Repairing bad credit takes patience and persistence. But you should have fewer negative marks to dispute on each successive round. A creditor, who responds promptly the first time, may not the second or third time. But remember, during the credit repair process; allow no new credit problems to appear on your credit record.

I have had problems correcting my credit record with one of the major bureaus. I find them difficult to work with. Any practical advice?

If you want better and faster results from the credit bureaus, follow these tactics:

1. Send your dispute letter to a different branch office of the same credit bureau, (particularly if you once lived in another part of the country). While you may need to justify the reasons to transfer your file to a new branch, this is usually easily accomplished. Simply state in your letter that you previously lived in that location or that the dispute originated there.

2. Send dispute letters to the 'Vice President of Customer Relations,' at the credit bureau. He or she has the power to investigate from the top down.

3. Establish a personal, friendly relationship with someone at the credit bureau. For example, if you receive correspondence from a specific individual at the credit bureau, direct your letters to that individual.

4. Notify the credit bureau's legal department – especially if there are obsolete or unverified entries which legally must be removed.

A credit bureau notified me that since a creditor verified a protested entry the negative mark shall remain on my credit report. I question whether this is true. What are my rights?

You can challenge whatever information is reported as 'confirmed' by the credit bureau. The FCRA states, "Every consumer reporting agency shall, upon request and proper identification of any consumer, clearly and accurately disclose to the consumer the sources of the information." You can therefore request the name, address, and phone numbers of those creditors who supposedly verified the information. If there is an intermediary – such as a collection agency – this will require additional time because the collection agency must contact the original creditor. But collection agencies seldom confirm this information because this time-consuming correspondence doesn't generate fees for them. Conversely, the creditor must spend time to gather information and send it to the collection agency. You are also entitled to an explanation of how the information was verified. For instance, verification by phoning the collection agency without contacting the creditor is insufficient proof of a debt. The credit bureau must prove that they first attempted to contact the creditor. And this is important because credit bureaus oftentimes do not attempt to obtain direct creditor verification.

My account has been turned over to a collection agency. Is it possible to negotiate with them to delete the negative entry?

Collection agencies frequently agree to delete a negative mark once you pay the original or settlement amount. Simply ask the collection agency, "Do you delete?"

Collection agencies frequently agree to delete a negative mark once you pay the original or settlement amount. Simply ask the collection agency, "Do you delete?" Some agencies will charge you a small deletion fee, but it's worth the small fee. Of course, you can reach the same agreement directly with your creditor.

I have paid a collection agency on an overdue account, but the collection item still appears on two of my credit reports. Suggestions?

Most collection agencies will give you a 'deletion letter' to indicate that your collection item has been deleted from their system. Unless you have this deletion letter, the credit bureaus can keep the collection item on your report for up to seven years. Once you send a deletion letter to all three credit bureaus, the collection item will be finally and forever removed.

If a credit bureau does not follow proper procedures, who can I complain to?

Contact the Federal Trade Commission. Or you can file a formal dispute with the Sub-Committee on Banking, Credit and Insurance. Unlike the Federal Trade Commission, this committee is interested in individual issues and problems in the credit reporting field. Send them your credit reports, correspondence between you and the credit bureau, and a full explanation of your problem. Direct your correspondence to the Subcommittee on Banking, Credit and Insurance, 2129 Rayburn House Office Building, Washington, DC 20515. (202) 225-4247.

I have successfully cleared my credit record with one credit bureau. Can I use this corrected record to correct my credit with the other two national bureaus?

Whenever you correct one credit report, send copies to the other credit bureaus to show that the negative entries were deleted

– assuming their credit reports show the same negative entries. Request that these credit bureaus also remove these same negative marks from their credit report. However, be certain that no other negative marks appear on your credit report which can damage you if they are disclosed to the other credit bureaus.

Can I pay a creditor to withdraw their negative credit mark from my credit report?

A creditor cannot withdraw an otherwise accurate negative mark, such as a 'late pay,' however a satisfied creditor may choose not to contest or verify a protest that you file. This, of course, will cancel the negative mark.

Creditors can cooperate in helping you to improve your credit rating. Write the creditor and explain how the problem arose. Be specific. Submit relevant details and documentation. Be factual, but also appeal to the creditor's sense of goodwill. Perhaps your company went bankrupt or you lost your job. Or perhaps you were detained in a foreign country on a business trip and therefore unable to punctually pay your account. Remind the creditor that you eventually paid and that you appreciated their services or products. Appeal to the creditor's compassion and ask their cooperation to remove the negative mark now that the account is settled.

Your letters to your creditors should be consistent so that whatever creditor comments appear on your credit file will also be consistent.

Personally interact with your creditors. If your first call to a creditor proves futile, don't be discouraged. Try again. Persist. Talk to a different individual. Large companies have many employees in their credit and customer relations department, and they may react differently to your situation. Eventually, someone may cooperate. And once a creditor agrees to change your credit report, have the creditor confirm it in writing.

For how long can negative marks stay on my credit report?

Credit bureaus generally report credit delinquencies for seven years. This includes reports of late and non-payments as well as collections or charge-offs. Most negative marks fall within the seven-year rule.

However, it can be difficult to determine when the seven year reporting period begins, and hence, becomes obsolete. The Federal Trade Commission says the time period runs from the date of the last activity on your account. But this date could be when you made your last payment – or later – such as when the creditor made its last collection effort. Once your creditor charged-off your account, you do not restart or extend the seven year period on reporting by making a subsequent payment.

While a credit bureau must generally delete adverse credit information that is over seven years old, the credit bureau can – without time limitation – disclose adverse credit information on credit transactions involving more than $50,000. For instance, a default on a $100,000 mortgage. There are other exceptions:

- *Life insurance over $50,000.* As with credit over $50,000, a credit bureau can report adverse credit information of any age to an insurance company checking your credit for a life insurance policy with a face value of $50,000 or more.

- *Employment with an annual salary over $20,000.* A credit bureau also can report credit information that is obsolete to a prospective employer who may offer you a job that pays more than $20,000 a year. Although a credit bureau can report obsolete credit information, credit bureaus normally do not report such outdated credit information.

- *Lawsuits and judgments.* Credit bureaus can report lawsuits and judgments against you for seven years from date of entry. However, this can be extended to whatever time period a judgment remains in force under state law. In many states, this extends for 20 years or more.

- *Bankruptcy.* Bankruptcy can remain on your credit record for 10 years from the date of filing (not the date of discharge). Credit bureaus usually report Chapter 13 wage-earner plans for seven years, and Chapter 7 bankruptcies for ten years.

- *Tax liens.* An unpaid IRS tax lien also can be reported for 10 years from the date of filing the lien. A paid tax lien can stay on your record for seven years from the date you made final payment.

- *Arrest, indictment or conviction.* Credit bureaus can report arrests, indictments or conviction of a crime for seven years from the date of disposition of the case, release or parole – whichever occurs last.

How do I get the credit bureau to delete old obsolete marks from my credit report?

Once you identify obsolete marks on your credit report, write the credit bureaus to delete them. Sample letters for this purpose are in this book.

Enforce your rights! If any entry is obsolete (beyond the time limit within which the

> Once you identify obsolete marks on your credit report, write the credit bureaus to delete them.

information can legally remain on your credit report), then the credit bureau *must* delete it from your record. Document your case so the credit bureau can quickly see that the information is obsolete. Show when the reporting period began so the credit bureau can readily determine that the information is obsolete and therefore must be deleted from your credit report.

The credit bureau should within 30 days acknowledge that it is deleting the obsolete information. Request an updated report to verify that the mark is deleted. If the credit bureau refuses to delete the obsolete information, threaten the bureau with a legal suit for damages and a complaint to the Federal Trade Commission. Be prepared to follow through. If the credit bureau does not reply within 30 days of your written request, you can then additionally demand deletion of the mark due to a late reply.

Which marks are most damaging to my credit?

While too many late-pay or no-pay entries on your credit report will seriously hurt your credit, the four greatest credit-killers are:

- Tax liens
- Foreclosures and repossessions
- Bankruptcy
- Outstanding judgments.

If any of these credit killers are on your credit report (and are current and accurate), you can still possibly have them removed. The strategy? Once again take advantage of the law that a credit bureau must verify disputed entries within 30 days, or delete the negative entry from your credit report.

This is how credit repair companies repair credit. Whenever a bankruptcy, tax lien, foreclosure or judgment appears on the credit report, they protest the entry and rely on the probability that the credit bureau cannot verify the information within 30 days. The bureau must then delete the information from the credit report.

Consider what happens in practice: Assume that you deny owing the IRS and therefore dispute their tax lien. The credit bureaus must have the IRS verify their information. However, after about two years, your tax records are probably stored in the federal archives, so the IRS may be unable to verify your tax liability within the required 30 days. The tax lien on your credit report must then be deleted (but the tax lien itself remains in force).

Then consider the many ways you have to dispute a foreclosure or repossession. Perhaps you only guaranteed the loan, or voluntarily surrendered the collateral to the lender, or you fully paid the loan balance so the lender incurred no loss. A foreclosure mark against you would then be misleading and disputable. The odds here are also good that the lender will not verify or defend the foreclosure entry.

If I pull my own credit report, will it count against me as an 'inquiry?'

No. When you request your own credit report, there is no negative consequence. You only have an 'inquiry' entered when a prospective creditor, mortgage

> When you request your own credit report, there is no negative consequence. You only have an 'inquiry' entered when a prospective creditor, mortgage lender, credit card issuer, etc., requests your credit report.

lender, credit card issuer, etc., requests your credit report. These inquiries stay on your record for two years. You can generally get up to six inquiries in a 30 day period before your score changes. You can, of course, provide prospective creditors copies of your credit report to reduce the number of inquiries.

I have several negative marks on my credit report that are at least three years old. How harmful are these old negative marks on my credit score?

Prospective creditors rarely look back seven years (the length of time a negative mark can stay on your record). They usually focus on the last 18 months. So old 'dings,' will be less harmful than newer 'dings.' That's why you should concentrate first on cleaning up those newer marks on your credit report.

Do prospective creditors know if I am 'maxed-out' on my credit cards?

Yes, And when you are at, or close to your credit limit on your credit cards, it can account for as much as 40 percent of a low credit score. Add a few late payments or collections and your credit score can really tumble.

My credit report continues to show a $6,000 loan balance on a two-year old loan where the balance has been reduced to $2,000. Will this hurt my credit?

Credit reports oftentimes show old balances. This is particularly true with car loans because many car lenders do not have computerized credit report updating to reflect new balances. Dispute every inaccurate high balance on your credit report. For fastest action, handle the dispute on-line or by phone. You may get an updated balance within one week.

If you show an old 'high balance' with MBNA Visa or American Express, wait for the next 30 day update. If it is not then updated (or you need a quick update), they will probably accommodate you within 48 hours.

If I divorce, can a creditor request a new credit application from me?

No. Unless one spouse refuses to pay or an account was opened based strictly on one spouse's income, a creditor cannot request a new credit application on a joint account or credit card simply due to divorce or separation.

I filed bankruptcy several years ago, but the bankruptcy never appeared on my credit report. Wouldn't it appear automatically?

Bankruptcies, liens, foreclosures and judgments are matters of public record. The public records list these entries by name and social security number. If the social security number on your credit report fails to match the public records, the debt cannot be identified. A simple error of even one digit of your social security number can prevent your bankruptcy from being identified. This is why many bankruptcies, liens and judgments fail to show up on credit reports. They do not match.

Conversely, someone else's bankruptcy, lien or judgment may erroneously end up on your credit report because of mistake in social security number. That is another reason why you must periodically check your credit record.

Can you always erase bankruptcy and other negative credit marks by taking advantage of the 30 day verification provision?

No. Erasing bad credit marks by taking advantage of the 30 day verification provision has its limitations. Government agencies – such as the IRS and the bankruptcy courts – were once 'paper' bureaucracies with a limited ability and incentive to swiftly reply to a credit bureau request for verification. But this is rapidly changing. Computerized records now make it far easier for governmental agencies to retrieve information and they now more frequently reply to credit challenges.

What impact does the new bankruptcy law have on credit consumers?

The new bankruptcy law contains many provisions that would benefit creditors. Most significant for creditors are provisions that will shift some debtors from Chapter 7 to Chapter 13 bankruptcy proceedings, as well as provisions that would expand the types of debts that would be non-dischargeable. By expanding the types of debts that are non-dischargeable, some creditors would continue to receive payments on debts that would previously be dischargeable. Means-testing in the bankruptcy system will likely result in more individuals being required to seek relief under Chapter 13, rather than Chapter 7. Because Chapter 13 requires debtors to develop a plan to repay creditors over a specified period, the pool of funds available for distribution for creditors will likely increase.

What other changes have been made concerning credit transactions under the new bankruptcy law?

There are several other important changes:

- ■ Credit lenders must provide additional disclosures to consumers in billing statements with respect to various open-end credit plans regarding the disadvantages of making only the minimum payment. Other disclosures would be required to be included in application and solicitation materials involving introductory rate offers, internet-based credit card solicitations, credit extensions secured by a dwelling and for late payment deadlines and penalties. Based on information from credit lenders, Federal bankruptcy judges have the authority to prohibit consumer reporting agencies from issuing a report containing any information relating certain involuntary bankruptcy petitions the court has dismissed.

- ■ The law would prohibit termination of a credit account before its expiration date because the consumer has not incurred finance charges.

What credit purchases will not be dischargeable in bankruptcy?

People who bought luxury goods or services in excess of $500 on credit or received cash advances within 90 days of the bankruptcy filing, may not have these debts discharged.

Should I contest all my negative marks simultaneously or scatter my protests over a period of time?

Challenge your entries separately and over time. If the credit bureau sees too many simultaneous and unrelated challenges at one time, the credit bureau will probably consider your protest frivolous. If the credit bureau has good reason to believe that your protest is frivolous or made in bad faith, it can disregard the 30-day rule. To avoid this, don't simultaneously challenge your negative entries. Challenge each individually. Finally, avoid form letters or boiler plate correspondence or that 'assembly line' approach to credit repair.

Once a credit bureau deletes a negative mark on my credit report, can the negative mark be restored?

No. Once a negative mark is deleted, it is forever deleted from the credit bureau's file. Neither the creditor nor the credit bureau can restore the negative mark to your record.

Once I fix incorrect information on my credit report how can I be certain it won't reappear?

You can't. While credit bureaus must have procedures in place to permanently eliminate corrected negative information from your credit report, sometimes these procedures fail.

To verify that your negative information remains deleted from your report, order a copy of your credit report 3 to 6 months after the item was first removed.

To verify that your negative infomation remains deleted from your report, order a copy of your credit report 3 to 6 months after the item was first removed.

Also check to see whether the same item was deleted at the other credit bureaus. Only through periodic review of your credit report can you be certain that the item remains deleted.

My husband is constantly in financial trouble. Will his negative credit history be reflected on my credit report?

It shouldn't. Whether you are single, married or divorced, your credit report should be limited to your credit information only. Information on both spouses can appear in both credit files only if both spouses can incur credit or are liable on an account. Joint accounts are an example.

How long will it take to fix my credit?

That depends on many factors. If you need to correct only one or two negative marks you may possibly accomplish this in under two months. On the other hand, it may take 24 to 36 months to enter enough favorable entries to your credit report to give you a high credit rating.

FOUR

HOW TO BUILD GREAT CREDIT

Just as you can turn poor credit into good credit, you can as easily turn good credit into great credit!

In the prior chapter you saw how to repair your credit. Of course, that is the all-important first step to great credit because it eliminates those negatives that identify you as a poor credit risk. But even when you accomplish this, you have only average or 'fair' credit. Your credit report may still not convince prospective creditors that you are a good credit risk, someone who deserves the credit you reasonably request – and on the best terms. You want more credit-power – the highest possible credit score!

How do prospective creditors measure my credit-power?

It starts with your FICO® score. If your FICO® score is under 720, you need to build your credit. But to measure your true credit power, a prospective creditor will also measure you against the 'three C's of credit':

1. 'Capacity,' or sufficient income to pay the debt,

2. 'Collateral,' or sufficient assets to secure the obligation, and

3. 'Character,' or willingness to promptly repay the debt.

I pay cash for nearly everything and as a result, have a low FICO® score. Shouldn't my ability to pay cash improve my credit score?

> An inadequate credit history can be as damaging as a poor credit history. Get a couple of credit cards to begin building a credit history.

No. Your problem is that you have an inadequate credit history and therefore, prospective creditors have less ability to foresee how you would handle credit. An inadequate credit history can be as damaging as a poor credit history. Get a couple of credit cards to begin building a credit history. Also, ask former creditors who have extended you credit in one form or another, to add their positive entries to your credit report.

To what extent does age influence credit scores?

Age is a definite factor. Older applicants have a decided advantage over those 30 or younger who are perceived as poorer credit risks.

How will a low FICO® score effect me?

It will adversely impact you in several ways.

1. You may be denied credit, or pay higher interest (APR) for any credit that you do get.

2. You may be denied employment or a promotion.

3. You may get less credit than you now have.

4. Your insurance rates may rise.

Does the FICO® scoring model give more weight to the credit usage on revolving accounts than on installment accounts?

Yes. One reason is that people have more flexibility with borrowing and repaying revolving accounts so their activity on revolving accounts is a better predictor of their bill paying habits. Installment loans require the same amount to be paid each month so installment accounts are less predictive of good money management habits. Therefore, installment accounts will less affect FICO® scores than will revolving accounts.

What if I usually hold my balance to about 50 percent of my credit line but occasionally make a large purchase that maxs my credit card. Does that hurt my FICO® score?

When you make a large purchase that maxs out your card it may temporarily lower your FICO® score, but your score should rebound once you pay down the balance to your customary utilization rate.

Bear in mind that your credit score is based on what is on your credit report the moment the score is calculated. So it may take a week or two for your credit score to change.

Will constantly maxing out my credit line hurt my FICO® score?

About 30 percent of your credit score is based on the following factors:

- Amount owed on specific types of accounts

- Number of accounts with balances

- Amount owed on all accounts
- Utilization rate (or proportion of credit line used to total credit available on revolving accounts)
- Utilization rate (or proportion of credit line used to total credit available on installment accounts)

If I only have one credit card – and max it out – will this hurt my FICO® score more than if I also have several other cards with available credit?

Definitely. Someone who has only one credit card and no other debts or credit activity will have their FICO® score lowered more when that credit card is fully utilized. Conversely, someone with several cards with a history of prompt payment and who typically keeps a low balance won't see much of a FICO® score change if they occasionally max out a card.

What is meant by a utilization rate?

This is the percent of credit you're using. When you close an account, you lower the amount of available credit – and with it, your utilization rate. This can adversely affect your credit score.

What has greater impact on my FICO® score my utilization rate per account or my aggregate utilization rate?

> Both factors – individual credit utilization and aggregate utilization – influence the FICO® score.

Both factors – individual credit utilization and aggregate utilization – influence the FICO® score. For that reason you don't want your utilization rate to be higher than 50 percent, whether on any one account, or in the aggregate on all accounts.

How does my 'capacity' or income play into the credit decision?

Prospective creditors, particularly lenders, want to know that you have enough income to repay the debt, and that your income exceeds your expenses so that you can *comfortably* pay the debt. So any lender will want to know that your total income (from every source), exceeds your fixed expenses, as well as your other debts and repayment obligations.

The net income you have available after deducting your fixed monthly expenses and other debts, is your repayment

> The net income you have available after deducting your fixed monthly expenses and other debts, is your repayment capacity.

capacity. If your net income (after taxes) is $2,000 a month and your total living expenses (rent, food, clothing, medical, etc.) is $1,500, then your credit capacity is whatever amount requires $500 or less per month to pay. If you pay $400 a month on other credit obligations, you have only $100 a month available, and a creditor should not extend you more credit than you can repay on $100 a month. To maximize your credit power, you must then either: 1) Increase your income; 2) decrease your expenses; or 3) reduce your other debts.

How can I show the highest possible income?

A higher income gives you more disposable income and capacity to pay debts. You also appear more stable or responsible than will a low-income earner. While this is not always true, a higher income nevertheless implies creditworthiness, at least within the credit industry.

While you cannot always get a higher paying job, you can boost your income by reporting overtime pay, bonuses and anticipated raises. And your salary is only one income source. Also disclose to prospective creditors commissions, interest, dividends, rents, royalties, alimony and support, governmental subsidies and social security. This extra income will boost your borrowing power.

You may have other overlooked income. For instance, do you expect repayment of a debt, an inheritance or settlement on a legal case? Creditors will be less willing to extend credit against this type of future income because it is less certain; however, reporting these and other potential income sources can tip the credit decision in your favor.

Do you plan to sell a major asset, such as a house, car or boat, to purchase something you want to finance? Let the creditor know that the loan will be fully or partly repaid from these proceeds rather than from your income.

Earnings are important, but so too is the stability of your income. Occupation is important to the extent it reflects earnings stability. Some occupations are more stable than others. For instance, a tenured teacher is considered to have a more secure employment future than does a construction worker or commissioned salesperson.

What other information on a credit application signals instability?

Your credit application also reflects financial instability if you live in a residence hotel, use a mail drop, are employed by a new business, have a recent drug conviction, are a non-citizen, have many recent address changes, or have too many credit cards for your income. Time on the job is another stability factor. Lenders want their credit applicants employed at the same job for at least one year, and also with a steady employment history for the prior five years.

Explain frequent job interruptions. Did you voluntarily leave your employment? Why? Were you self-employed during these intervals? Were you unemployed due to a business closing? Don't leave these issues unanswered. Creditors want to know that you will have that steady income to pay your obligations. Need a long term loan? Convince the lender that your job has long-term stability. Is your employer a small business? Encourage your lender to check its financial stability. Self-employed? Show the lender your business' financials. Plan to change jobs? Apply for credit before you leave your present employer.

Few credit applications give you adequate space to fully explain your job history. Attach a brief explanation, for instance, if you changed jobs frequently or if your position was terminated due to plant shutdown, a return to school, a military stint, medical problem or you have similar explanations that reflect favorably on you as an employee.

I have heard having finance companies listed on my credit report can actually lower my score even if I paid them promptly. True?

Finance companies can appear to be 'lenders-of-last-resort' to other prospective creditors. As such, you may get a lower score only because you have a credit history with one or two finance companies.

I earn over $90,000 annually but still have limited credit. Several lenders and credit card companies have suggested that my expenses are too high. How can I correct this?

Credit applications require you to list your major expenses. When your expenses are excessive for your income, you won't have sufficient funds to repay loans. In other words, you have no credit capacity.

Reconstruct your monthly budget. How much money do you have remaining after you pay your living expenses? If you cannot significantly increase your income, how can you reduce your expenses to increase your credit capacity? Where can you economize and lower your expenses? What expenses can others share? What expenses will soon end (college tuition, etc.)?

Lenders use different yardsticks to determine whether you are carrying too much debt. Most lenders want your monthly debt payments (exclusive of your mortgage payment) to stay under 20 percent of your gross or pre-tax income. For example, if your gross income is $5,000 a month, a lender will not want your other debts payments to exceed $1,000. But that is only a rough rule-of-thumb. Lenders will also consider your monthly expenses, whether your income will increase, whether other debts will soon be paid, and whether you historically carried that amount of debt and still promptly paid your obligations. Of course, it is best to apply for new credit after you have paid down your present obligations. New lenders will be more hesitant to give you more credit when you are already heavily indebted.

Never omit debts from your credit application. Lenders check your credit reports. 'Omitted' credit accounts that appear on your report will only throw into question your honesty and integrity, which will hurt your chances for credit. If you delete an account from your credit application, then review your credit reports beforehand to make certain the 'omitted account' does not appear; and disclose those accounts that do appear.

What other 'rules of thumb' tell me if I have too much debt?

Prospective creditors and lenders apply countless ratios to determine whether you are over-indebted, or whether you still have a credit capacity.

One common example is the 10 percent rule used by lenders to determine the amount you can safely handle in monthly payments. They frequently apply this yardstick to new applicants. Under this rule, your monthly payments should not exceed 10 percent of your monthly net income. If your monthly net income is $1,500, your total monthly loan payments should not exceed $150.

The 28 percent rule is used for home mortgages. Your monthly mortgage payments should not exceed 28 percent of your gross income. This rule is useful when you have no other debts, such as credit card debts or automobile loans that detract from your credit capacity.

There is also the 36 percent rule. This states that your mortgage, combined with all other debts, should not exceed 36 percent of your annual gross income. This is not the monthly payments, but your total debt.

Won't my credit rating and other credit factors become less important if I give a creditor adequate collateral to secure a loan?

Possibly. The answer depends on the lender. Some asset-based lenders depend primarily on the value of their collateral and are less concerned about credit rating. Banks and other conventional lenders, on the other hand, want both collateral and creditworthiness.

> A lender can either be secured or unsecured. Secured creditors have a lien against specific assets, such as real estate, a car, or boat. If you fail to pay, the secured lender can sell the pledged asset to recover payment.

A lender can either be secured or unsecured. Secured creditors have a lien against specific assets, such as real estate, a car, or boat. If you fail to pay, the secured lender can sell the pledged asset to recover payment. This is the safest loan for a lender, provided the pledged asset can be sold by the lender for the amount necessary to cover the loan balance. Secured lenders loan against the auction value of the collateral.

Secured credit is an almost guaranteed way to rebuild your credit. Even with poor credit, a lender may give you credit if you can secure the credit with a lien against some valuable asset. Many asset-based lenders extend credit entirely on the strength of the pledged assets, though you are likely to pay higher finance charges for the loan.

If you have bad credit you can try to rebuild your credit through a series of secured loans. Once you establish your creditworthiness on these secured obligations, you become a good candidate for an unsecured loan.

Unsecured creditors, of course, are less protected than secured creditors. An unsecured lender cannot seize an asset if you fail to pay. They must first sue on their claim and win a

THE ABC's OF CREDIT • **103**

judgment. Only then can the lender seize your assets. However, if you have no assets, or if your assets have previously been pledged to other lenders, then an unsecured lender has little recourse to collect, notwithstanding the judgment. Still, unsecured creditors do consider your assets. Unsecured creditors see significant assets as a sign of financial stability. And when your assets significantly exceed your liabilities, the lender has sufficient assets to satisfy any judgment.

I own a $300,000 home with a $180,000 mortgage, and want a credit line to build my business. What assets can I pledge as collateral?

Any collateral can be used to secure your loan and build your credit. And you may be wealthier than you think. Add up the value of all your assets and subtract the mortgages or liens against

> Any collateral can be used to secure your loan and build your credit. And you may be wealthier than you think. Add up the value of all your assets and subtract the mortgages or liens against those assets. The difference is your equity.

those assets. The difference is your equity. This is what you have available to secure a loan. Don't overlook any asset, or the equity remaining in your home, investment real estate, stocks, bonds, mutual funds, automobile, boats, planes, recreational vehicles, notes and mortgages due you, art, jewelry, antiques, pensions, IRAs Keoghs, etc.

Other assets can be pledged. Your collateral gives you borrowing power equal to the amount of your equity. Regardless of your credit history, if your collateral is worth $100,000, you can always borrow nearly that amount. Consider your assets current value, not what you paid for it. Lenders, of course, prefer liquid assets as collateral, (a pledged bankbook or securities), because these assets are more easily liquidated. However, many lenders lend against homes, automobiles or other tangible assets.

I understand that some people increase their paper net worth and improve their credit rating by buying stock in their own corporation and giving it an inflated value on their credit application. How does this work?

Some people applying for credit have been known to increase their net worth by setting up their own corporation (which, in some states, can be done for less than $100). The corporation then issues private stock, which is then listed on a credit application at a greatly inflated value. Since there is no public trading on the stock, most lenders will accept the stated value without further investigation. This is not a recommended strategy because it is a deceptive borrowing practice.

You say 'character' is important in the credit decision. How is 'character' evaluated?

In the credit world, 'character' means the probability that you will honor your future obligations. This is based on how you have paid your past obligations. However, creditors look beyond past credit history. They also want to know more about you: How many credit defaults have you had and what were the reasons for the defaults?

Do you own your own home? If you rent, for how long have you rented the same apartment or house? Do you have a checking account and savings account? Do you make regular deposits? Do you maintain a payroll savings plan at work? Do you have a telephone in your own name? Do you have a criminal record? Have you filed bankruptcy? Stability essentially translates into 'character' in credit parlance.

Through these questions, prospective creditors see patterns. A creditor won't find that negative pattern if you have few recent credit defaults, or if you owned your own home for a number of years despite financial difficulties, or recently purchased a home and promptly made every mortgage payment, or rented at the same location for a number of years. Creditors also consider a checking and savings account funded with regular deposits a significant sign of financial stability.

Positive indicators can often offset negative credit information. Obviously, it will also depend a great deal on how good your credit is now. Essentially, a lender must believe that you will remain in town to repay your loan, that you practice sound credit management, and that you are stable, responsible, and productive.

I have good credit and yet I have been denied credit on several occasions. Am I entitled to know why my credit application was rejected?

Whenever you're denied credit, the Equal Credit Opportunity Act (ECOC) entitles you to know the reasons why. If the creditor doesn't supply you with the reasons, ask. Here are the 20 most common reasons for credit rejection:

1. Credit application was incomplete.

2. Too few credit references.

3. Credit references could not be verified.

4. No credit file.

5. Credit file had insufficient information.

6. Delinquent credit obligations.

7. Not employed for an adequate period.

8. Employment irregular.

9.   Employment cannot be verified.

10. Insufficient income.

11. Income cannot be verified.

12. Excess debts.

13. Insufficient collateral.

14. Lived too briefly at present address.

15. Current residence temporary.

16. Current residence cannot be verified.

17. Wages are currently garnished or attached.

18. Foreclosure, tax liens, bankruptcy, or repossession on recent record.

19. The creditor does not grant credit on the terms requested or offer the type loan requested. (Don't apply to a lender unless you are certain that the creditor offers the type credit you want. You will only incur an unnecessary inquiry on your credit record).

20. Credit score too low.

These only highlight the many possible obstacles to credit. If you foresee one or more of these problems, then attach a note of explanation to your application.

What can I do if my credit application was denied?

You can appeal to a prospective creditor once you know why your credit was rejected. Candidly discuss the problem with the creditor. Most creditors will tell you what you can do to qualify for credit. Don't be antagonistic. Remember, the prospective creditor only wants to know that you are creditworthy and can repay the debt. Be both persistent and concerned about why your application was not approved. Also remember that a prospective creditor may approve a request for *less* credit, or give you credit on somewhat different terms than you proposed on your application. Explore every alternative!

I recently divorced and have no personal credit history. How can I build my own credit?

In this case, a first step to building credit is to open your own checking and savings account at a local bank or credit union. Select a bank that reports credit transactions to the credit bureaus. Secondly, open utility accounts in your name. Gas, electric and telephone bills paid monthly and reported to the credit bureaus will also help to establish credit. Third, try to obtain modest credit. If necessary, use your savings account as collateral to borrow dollar-for-dollar on a passbook loan. You can borrow as little as $500. Once you secure a loan with a passbook, you cannot, of course, access the funds until you fully repay the loan, so be certain you will not need these funds for at least 30 days. A bank secured with your passbook has no lending risk. But it is important that the bank or credit union report your consumer loan to the credit bureau. If your bank will not, find another bank. These simple credit builders will add good marks to your credit report.

Once you do borrow, repay the loan within 25 days. When you fully repay the loan before the due date, the bank or credit union will send a positive entry to your credit bureau. Finally, continue to deposit regularly to your savings account to build your balance and qualify for more credit.

What if my credit is poor but I have a relative with strong credit. Can my relative help me to build my credit?

A trusted friend or relative with good credit and a bank card can request that their bank issue a second card in your name. This second card issued to you will have a different account number, and the original signer of the account will be the guarantor. The credit bureau will then report the entire history of the original card's credit transactions on your report. The credit history will include the date the account was opened and the entire payment record. However, it will not indicate that your credit report is based on a secondary card. Your credit report then will remain completely independent and reflect excellent credit. If your bank asks you to complete a credit application for the secondary card, then have the cardholder complete it as the co-applicant.

The use of both secured credit cards and cosigners can help you to establish credit. Borrow and repay promptly and you will win more credit. But try to obtain credit only from those lenders who will report your prompt payments to credit bureaus, because this is how these positive credit entries will land on your credit report.

How important is it that my lenders report my credit limit to the credit bureaus?

Your FICO® score is heavily based on your amount of revolving debt compared to the total line of credit available. This is your debt-to-credit limit. As your debt increases against your credit limit, your FICO® score will fall. For this reason you should ask your lenders to report your credit limit; particularly when you carry low balances.

Can I request that my good credit history be added to my credit report?

Yes, and you should. Frequently, student loans, merchant cards and other credit arrangements are not reported to the three

> Frequently, student loans, merchant cards and other credit arrangements are not reported to the three credit bureaus.

credit bureaus. It's simple to accomplish. Write your creditor, make reference to your account, and request that it be added to your credit file.

My prior bankruptcy has been on my credit file for nearly ten years. Won't my FICO® score increase once the 10 year reporting period expires and the bankruptcy is deleted from my credit file?

Not necessarily. In fact, deleting your bankruptcy may actually lower your FICO® score. Here's why. Your FICO® score model has 10 groups. With bankruptcy on your record, you are grouped and ranked with other prior bankrupts. When your bankruptcy is deleted, you will be moved and ranked against another group of non-bankrupts, and your credit history, comparatively, may then appear less attractive.

Can you remove bankruptcy from a credit report?

Bankruptcy is difficult to remove from a credit report but it is nevertheless possible. For example,

> Bankruptcy is difficult to remove from a credit report but it is nevertheless possible.

you may have filed a Chapter 13 wage-earner plan or Chapter 11 reorganization (which differs from Chapter 7 bankruptcy). You can then challenge a 'bankruptcy' entry. You must take advantage of these technicalities. As with the IRS, the bankruptcy courts also archive their old files after a year or two, and cannot always easily verify their information within 30 days. But do remove your other negative marks before you attempt to remove a bankruptcy mark. If you can remove the negative creditor marks that were discharged in your bankruptcy, the bankruptcy itself would be less verifiable and more easily removed.

Will it help my FICO® score if I pay an old delinquent debt that appears on my credit file?

It sometimes does more harm than good because the creditor may report your payment on the old debt as a new account activity. This will lower your FICO® score because new activities are weighed more heavily than older transactions. Your negative information (the delinquency) is then moved to the forefront of your credit history.

Will it hurt my credit rating to have available credit that I do not use?

It can possibly hurt your credit because some prospective creditors may believe you would then go on a credit binge and draw down your credit. On the other hand, if you don't have a high credit line, it may signify that other prospective creditors do not see you as creditworthy.

I have several old and relatively inactive accounts on my credit history. Will it help or hurt my FICO® score to close these accounts?

Don't close old accounts that are in good standing. It will hurt your credit rating because it shortens your credit history and

> Don't close old accounts that are in good standing. It will hurt your credit rating because it shortens your credit history and thus decreases your average account age.

thus decreases your average account age. When you close these accounts you also lower your available credit which correspondingly increases your debt-to-credit limit. This will lower your FICO® score.

What debt-to-credit ratio should I try to maintain?

Keep your account balances at no more than 50 percent of your credit line (available credit). Many people have low FICO® scores only because they have high balances against their credit line.

Should I then open more credit lines to spread my debt and reduce my debt-to-credit limit?

Opening too many accounts is another way to damage your FICO® score. You want no more than five open credit lines at any time.

What is the best way to use revolving bank credit cards?

Carry two cards – one with no annual fee for purchases you pay in full each month and another that charges the lowest APR for revolving credit.

Will it help my FICO® score if I pay down my home equity loan?

When you discharge or significantly reduce your home equity loan, you can dramatically improve your FICO® score by 50 points or more, because you simultaneously decrease your debt-to-credit limit.

I heard about credit rescoring through a mortgage lender. How does this work and can it improve my FICO® score?

If you are seeking a new mortgage, you may qualify for credit rescoring which can help remove negative marks from your credit file. Essentially, a mortgage lender confirms to the credit bureaus that any outstanding tax liens, delinquent accounts, etc. have been paid. This will quickly delete these negative items from your credit file and improve your credit score.

I have several duplicate items on my credit report. Will this hurt my FICO® score, and how can I get them removed?

Always have the credit bureaus delete duplicate items which only lower a FICO® score. How do duplicate entries occur? For example, a lender may sell a loan which then appears on your credit file under both the original and new lenders name. It then appears that you have twice the actual amount of debt outstanding. This is another reason to frequently check your credit report.

My name is on my parents' credit card and since they have a long history of financial problems, my own credit is a mess. Solutions?

Your goal is to remove your name from their account to disassociate their credit problems from your own credit history. Assuming that you are only an authorized user and that the card is not in your name as the actual cardholder, the process should

THE ABC's OF CREDIT • **113**

be relatively easy. Have your parents call or write the credit card issuer and request that your name be deleted from their account. Follow up to make certain that your name has been removed. Once your name is removed as an authorized user, this should be reflected on your credit report within 30 days. Wait another 60-90 days to see whether your FICO® score improves. It should.

My spouse and I want to buy a home together, but my wife's FICO® score is only 480, while mine is over 800. How will our opposite credit ratings influence the mortgage we can obtain?

It commonly happens that two or more credit applicants on the same loan have polar FICO® scores. The best advice? Only the spouse with the higher score

> Only the spouse with the higher score should apply for the mortgage, otherwise the lender will average the scores, which will significantly increase the loan's interest rate.

should apply for the mortgage, otherwise the lender will average the scores, which will significantly increase the loan's interest rate.

My husband died recently. He handled most of the family finances and he had the stronger credit history. Can I continue to rely upon my husband's credit or should I now establish my own credit?

Establish your own credit – and do it as soon as possible. Most creditors will reduce or terminate your credit once they learn of your husband's death. Certainly, it is wisest to establish your own credit during your spouse's lifetime.

I am divorced and have re-adopted my maiden name. How do I transfer my credit history to my current name?

If you have had a credit history under another name you can transfer your credit history to your new name simply by notifying each of the credit bureaus (and also provide your new address, etc., if applicable). You should also directly contact your creditors of your name change. Similarly, if you move, notify the credit bureaus and your creditors.

I live in a community property state. How does my spouse's credit then affect my own?

Arizona, California, Idaho, Louisiana, Nevada, New Mexico, Texas and Washington are all community property states and follow community property law. Under these laws the prospective creditors of one spouse may consider the credit of the other spouse – even when credit is applied for in individual names. So, if you live in one of these states, it is important to encourage your spouse to maintain good credit.

How can I teach my children about the proper use of credit?

One way is to ask their school to request a presentation on avoiding credit card pitfalls from Credit Abuse Resistance Education (CARE). This organization now offers credit education programs for children in 28 states and are expanding. Contact CARE at (585) 613-4290.

I check the web to shop the best loan rates. Will this impact my credit score?

Possibly. If you actually apply for loans, the prospective lenders will check your credit and these excessive credit inquiries will hurt your FICO® score. Also be

> If you actually apply for loans, the prospective lenders will check your credit and these excessive credit inquiries will hurt your FICO® score.e.

careful when you shop for a new car. Car dealers frequently pull credit reports on prospective customers without their knowledge, and each credit check will count as an inquiry.

Won't Fair Isaac distinguish between shopping for a single loan versus shopping for a lot of new credit?

They try to. That is why it is best to shop for a loan over the shortest time span possible. A flurry of inquiries would indicate that you are shopping for a loan, while staggered inquiries over a longer time period may be interpreted as hunting new credit sources.

I have several late payments on my credit report because my payments arrived a day or two late. How can I avoid this in the future?

Mail your payments a few days early. Or pay your credit cards online or via telephone. Your payment will then be instantaneously posted and you will avoid delinquencies on your record and a lowered FICO® score.

Where can I go to get more information on how to improve my FICO® score?

Go to *myfico.com*. It has instructions for improving credit scores.

To what extent will adding personal information to my credit report help my credit?

It can greatly add to how creditors perceive your stability. For example, previous employment is important, particularly if you had your present job for less than two years. Your date of birth reflects your age, which can also be important. Similarly, list your prior residence if you have a new address.

What can I do to improve my credit rating if my accounts are now delinquent or have been turned over for collection?

Even delinquencies can be turned into a positive credit rating. Approach your creditors and negotiate repayment plans that sincerely demonstrate that you will make regular payments and revive their interest in you as a customer. In return you want your creditors to help restore your credit rating.

If your account is now with a collection agency, deal first with your creditor. Remember, collection agencies are not sales-oriented, and they are more difficult to negotiate with. So, try to avoid having your debt turned over for collection. But whether you negotiate with a collection agency or creditor, make it a 'win-win' offer. Your goal is to trade your payment for a positive credit rating. Negotiate a payment schedule in exchange for the creditor's promise to help you improve your credit rating. For example, you might offer full payment over 12 months if the creditor agrees to reward this commitment with a better credit mark. Be specific. Perhaps after three months of punctual payments your negative mark could be raised to a non-rating, or after six months of prompt payments your non-rating lifted to a positive rating. You see the idea?

Also negotiate for 'open account' status. It damages your credit if, despite your regular payments, your account remains closed to further purchases. So, ask your creditor to reopen your account for limited credit while you uphold your end of the agreement.

Do make certain that whatever terms you agree to fit your budget so you faithfully keep your promise. And put it in writing. If possible, make your payments ahead of schedule. If your ability to make payments is threatened by unemployment or illness, inform your creditor immediately.

Finally, verify your credit upgrade. Order an updated copy of your credit file to verify that the creditor has honored his side of the agreement and made the promised changes. If the agreed changes are not made, you can effectively dispute the information on your credit report by submitting a copy of the creditor-signed agreement to support the change.

My spouse has excellent credit and I am on many of the listed accounts jointly with my spouse. How can I have these favorable accounts reflected on my credit report?

Ask the creditors on these joint accounts to submit their information to your personal credit file. Of course, you can always ask a prospective creditor to consider a favorable joint credit reference, even when it does not appear on your credit file.

I have good credit with a number of 'non-reporting' accounts. How can I get these accounts listed on my credit report to bolster my rating?

The FTC has advised credit bureaus that where a credit report has resulted in unfavorable action against a credit consumer, the credit consumer should be able to add favorable accounts to the report to create a more complete and balanced picture of his or her repayment history. Consequently, the credit bureaus will, for a small fee (usually charge $2 to $3 per item), contact these creditors and add their information to your file. If you believe these positive accounts will offset negative entries on your report (or that it will complete an otherwise incomplete report), it is well worth the time and small investment.

Call every non-reporting creditor with whom you have a good credit relationship. Once they agree to release your account record, inform them which credit bureau will contact them. Then contact the credit bureau with the names of the non-reporting creditors, and ask the credit bureau to contact each creditor and add their information to your credit report as soon as the information is verified. By clearing your credit report of as many negative items as possible, and adding every positive item, you should greatly improve your credit score.

Several credit counselors have told me that filing bankruptcy can actually improve my credit rating. Is this true?

Many credit managers consider bankruptcy a positive sign, provided they believe that you are not a chronic credit risk. With bankruptcy they then consider your financial problems behind you, and they are mindful that you cannot again file for bankruptcy (Chapter 7) within 8 years. (You can, however, repeatedly file Chapter 11 or Chapter 13 bankruptcy.) Moreover, one negative mark (your bankruptcy) can be less damaging to your credit rating than will a large number of negative marks that will appear on your credit record if you do not file bankruptcy.

Are credit repair companies regulated?

Yes. The Federal Credit Repair Organization Act regulates for-profit credit repair companies (which explains why so many are set up as 'non-profits'). Several states further regulate their credit repair clinics.

What is the best way to finance a new car when I have poor credit?

Even with poor credit, or no credit, there are several ways to finance good transportation. Anyone can say goodbye to their broken down heap, and finance a vehicle they can proudly drive, even when they have little or no down payment and poor credit.

Credit unions are most lenient on new car loans. Join a credit union, then apply for a loan. But candidly explain any outstanding credit problems.

> Credit unions are most lenient on new car loans. Join a credit union, then apply for a loan. But candidly explain any outstanding credit problems.

Credit unions are more interested in your current financial situation, than your past credit problems. Both banks and credit unions require a down payment of about 25 percent of the price of the car. If you can afford this down payment, and can afford the monthly payments, you can probably finance a new car from a credit union, even when you have shaky credit.

If you are refused credit by both the banks and credit unions, then try to get credit from the car dealer. Select a large dealer within your area. Finance companies work with every car dealer, but the larger dealers have greater financing leverage. Car manufacturers operate their own finance companies to help their dealers sell more cars – and faster. A dealer who can offer instant financing through a manufacturer sponsored finance company can make the sale without the customer leaving the showroom. Many different financing arrangements are available to dealers, so even customers with a spotty credit record have good prospects for auto dealer financing.

Larger dealers create huge profits to their affiliated finance companies, and these larger dealers oftentimes get preferred treatment, including credit approval on more questionable loans. If the car you select matches what you can afford – you will probably get financed.

Before you do select your car, ask the salesman or credit manager about the down payment and interest rate as both will be based upon your credit rating. Their finance company will give the credit manager their minimum terms, but some dealers charge a higher interest rate and pocket the difference. So, negotiate the price of the car, and the interest rate and down payment. If you tried to finance through a bank or credit union, you have some basis for comparison, even if you were rejected. Remember, the dealer wants to sell or lease cars, and they have more experience with poor credit applicants than do traditional lenders. With poor credit you won't win great financing, but nevertheless, you may find the car that meets your needs on terms you can afford.

Won't a cosigner make it easier to get a car loan?

Financing any purchase is always easier when you have a creditworthy cosigner. A cosigner pledges his good credit for your loan. Lenders will overlook your poor credit when your cosigner's credit is strong. However, if you default, you risk the cosigner's good credit. Reduce your cosigner's risk. Buy term life insurance to cover the loan and protect the cosigner should you die or become disabled. Also make a larger down payment and pay your installments through your cosigner to better safeguard your cosigner.

If I can't find a cosigner, can I have a friend buy a car for me in his own name?

It is an option but it has several downsides. First, this arrangement won't help you build your own credit. Your friend can also have personal liability for your accidents, so make certain that you are well insured. Finally, because you are paying the car loan, consider how you will protect your equity in the vehicle which is titled to your friend. For example, what will happen if your friend gets divorced or files bankruptcy?

> Because you are paying the car loan, consider how you will protect your equity in the vehicle which is titled to your friend. For example, what will happen if your friend gets divorced or files bankruptcy?

How can some car dealers guarantee financing to buyers with poor credit?

The dealer guarantees the loan. If you default, the bank can recover from the dealer which then assumes the loan and repossesses your car. Dealer financing always requires higher interest. Another financing technique for used cars buyers with poor credit is the 'Buy-Here, Pay-Here' pitch. Used cars have higher profit margins than new ones, so a dealer can more easily finance a used car's full price. Your down payment covers the dealer's cost and your future payments become the dealer profit. This type financing is particularly common with lower-priced cars, nevertheless some dealers sell current model cars the same way.

Check 'Blue Book' car prices. This is the guide that banks and car dealers use to determine a vehicle's wholesale value. Any bank can also give you this price information. Know approximately what a 'Buy-Here, Pay-Here' dealer paid for the car you're interested in before you negotiate!

Should I buy credit life insurance on my car loan?

Usually not. This is very expensive term life insurance, and it is a costly way to repay your car loan if you die. Dealers push this insurance because it is so profitable, but it is illegal for a dealer to insist that you buy this insurance as a condition for financing. If you do want car loan life insurance, buy it from an outside insurance agency. You might save 50 percent or more.

Is car leasing a better alternative to owning and financing?

The answer depends on many factors. Leasing is increasingly popular. How does leasing differ from traditional financing? You finance a car to purchase it. Once you repay your loan, you own the car. When you lease a car you pay to use the car. You never own it. During the lease you pay for the car's maintenance and upkeep. You cannot sell it. At the end of the lease (usually 2 to 5 years) you return the car, unless you exercise an option to purchase the car. This option privilege, of course, must be stated in your car lease.

One leasing advantage is that your monthly payments may be slightly lower than if you financed-to-buy the car. Regardless of its selling price, you pay only for the depreciation on the car during the lease. For example, if your $15,000 car is worth $6,000 in five years, it depreciates 60 percent over the lease. Your lease payments are then based upon this $9,000 depreciation. This, together with interest, and dealer profit is paid monthly over the lease. Monthly lease payments then are generally lower than monthly finance charges because the financed amount is lower.

A variation to traditional leasing is to find someone who presently leases a car but wants out of the lease, which you would then assume. You can find such 'lease takeover' deals in the classifieds, but understand that every car lease requires that you get approval from the leasing company to assume the lease.

Companies specialize in lease takeover deals. You lease from them and they pay on the original lease. The original leaseholder remains liable to the leasing company. Examine their contracts carefully. These companies are also listed in the classifieds automotive section.

Whether you can credit-qualify for a car lease depends upon the economy. Surprisingly, it is easier to get credit in a tough economy when dealers are under more pressure to sell cars. A car lease may also require a substantial down payment or deposit, but as with any financing, the larger your down payment, the lower your lease payments.

I plan to buy a home soon but have a low FICO® score. Will I still be able to get a bank mortgage?

Bank lenders are conservative and have strict lending and qualifying requirements. Banks generally don't give mortgages to poor credit risks. Moreover, they frequently sell their mortgage to Fannie Mae and other investor groups who have even stricter credit requirements and are even more risk adverse.

Credit unions are more lenient than traditional banks. Be-

> Credit unions are more lenient than traditional banks. Besides your past credit history, they will also consider your current financial situation, ability to pay and financial stability.

sides your past credit history, they will also consider your current financial situation, ability to pay and financial stability. While every lender will consider your credit scores, you can explain your credit problems to these lenders.

I am applying for a mortgage and I understand that there is a 'Rapid Re-score' program that can help me to improve my credit rating. How does this work?

Mortgage brokers have access to a service called Factual Data. They charge about $25 to remove each negative mark on your credit report. The Rapid Re-score program through Factual Data may markedly improve your credit score within one week. However, you can only access this service through a mortgage broker.

Will I improve my credit score if I pay off the mortgage on my home?

Probably not. The credit bureaus do not differentiate between credit consumers who have heavy mortgages and those whose homes are debt-free. While home ownership is a definite plus, an outstanding mortgage is usually not a minus.

If I am denied a mortgage from a conventional lender, should I hire a mortgage broker?

Mortgage brokers are financial matchmakers between lender and borrower. Mortgage brokers represent countless banks, lending institutions, organizations, and private individuals with money to loan. The National Association of Mortgage Brokers estimate that their members handle about 50 percent of all mortgages. An experienced mortgage broker can assess your chances of getting a mortgage, identify your best sources, help with the mortgage application and negotiate interest and other loan terms. But you pay for this expertise and convenience. Mortgage brokers charge a fee of between 2 to 5 percent of the loan amount. To find a good mortgage broker, have your real estate agent refer you to one. But ask four questions to any mortgage broker: 1) How many lenders do you represent? (A good broker will represent at least 10 banks nationwide.) 2) What is their closing ratio? (70 percent is good.) 3) Can they supply local references? (Check thoroughly.) 4) What do they charge?

Do the Federal Housing Administration and Veterans Associations have more lenient credit policies than other lenders?

The FHA and the VA are insurers, not lenders. They guarantee your loan (or part of the loan) in case you default. If you credit qualify, you can get an FHA loan with only 5 percent down. You can

> The FHA and the VA are insurers, not lenders. They guarantee your loan (or part of the loan) in case you default. If you credit qualify, you can get an FHA loan with only 5 percent down. You can get a VA mortgage with no down payment.

get a VA mortgage with no down payment. To find out if you qualify for a FHA mortgage, contact a real estate broker, local bank, credit union or FHA directly.

A VA mortgage is available only to qualifying veterans. One who actively served for at least 90 days during World War II, the Korean or Vietnam War, or for at least 180 consecutive days before September 7, 1980, or served actively for at least 24 months after September 7, 1980.

Unlike an FHA mortgage, a VA mortgage only guarantees loans up to $36,000. The VA and the FHA both have assumable mortgages, which enable you to take over a seller's mortgage.

There are two types of assumable mortgages: Qualifying assumable mortgages are similar to traditional mortgages from traditional lenders. You must meet their specific requirements to qualify for a loan. Non-qualifying assumable mortgages require only that you can meet the monthly payments.

I have had poor credit for many years. Can you suggest alternate financing techniques to finance a home?

You have other options to home financing. Here are several:

1. *Owner financing.* A home seller will oftentimes finance the buyers. The seller receives a monthly income and can foreclose on the home if the buyer defaults. Owners who are anxious to sell frequently self-finance. Other sellers finance as an investment. If the seller has a mortgage on the home, the seller's mortgage becomes a second or junior mortgage.

2. *State financing agencies.* You may get low-interest home financing through your state's financing agency that is funded through mortgage revenue bonds. The down payment requirements can be less than 5 percent, and some state programs 100 percent finance.

3. *Equity sharing.* Would an investor buy and finance your home? You occupy the home, pay the mortgage, maintain the home and agree to lease the home for a specified time. Once you can afford to buy the home, you reimburse the investor together with a profit.

4. *Ask for your employer's help.* More and more companies finance their employees' down payment to buy a home. The repayment is deducted from the employees' wages. Or your employer may buy the home and lease it to you with an

option to buy. (Yes. An employer can get tax benefits from home ownership.)

5. *Form a syndicate*. Can you organize a group to invest? They would be collectively secured by your mortgage and also earn interest plus some equity from your property's appreciation.

6. *Pay the seller a financing bonus*. In exchange, negotiate lower interest and longer term loan to keep your monthly payments to about what it would be with a larger down payment. While you will pay the seller more over the term of your loan, you will pay less per month.

7. *Union financing*. The AFL-CIO, for instance, gives first time home loans to affiliated union members (with 3 percent or less down). Other union financing programs do not charge loan origination fees.

8. *Find probate properties*. Those who inherit homes may want to sell quickly and pocket their money. Heirs can be highly motivated sellers, especially if they must make mortgage payments on the home. They may then sell with little or no cash down terms to buyers with shaky credit.

I need about $500,000 to open a restaurant; however I have been told that I have too few assets to borrow this amount. Any tips?

You will find it far easier to finance a 'going' business than a start-up because an existing business has a track record and assets. Business lenders are asset-based so the assets of the business serve as collateral. Conversely, a business 'idea' is risky.

> You will find it far easier to finance a 'going' business than a start-up because an existing business has a track record and assets.

You must then convince someone to finance your idea. Unless you have the track record and experience to turn ideas into a successful business, you will find financing extremely difficult. Financing an existing business is, of course, far more complex than a home mortgage or car loan.

To succeed, choose the right bank. Banks specialize. So go to commercial banks. (Home mortgages and consumer loans are best obtained from savings banks and cooperatives.) If you need a small loan (under $100,000) apply at a small, local bank, as local banks are close to their customers and more actively support small, community-based businesses. Best bet: Approach the bank where the business has an existing banking relationship.

If my credit is too poor for outside financing to buy a business, how feasible is seller financing?

> Seller financing is often your best money source to buy a business. Many financial experts will advise you to ignore other lending sources until the seller has given his final 'no.'

Seller financing is often your best money source to buy a business. Many financial experts will advise you to ignore other lending sources until the seller has given his final 'no.' Seller financing features five big advantages:

First, sellers are less 'interest-hungry.' Sellers do not finance to earn interest. They finance to sell their business. A seller may finance you at lower interest, yet at a higher rate than the seller could earn on his money from a bank. Thus, the seller profits from his loan.

Second, sellers will usually wait longer for their money. Banks want business loans repaid within five years. However, a longer loan will reduce your payments and less strain your cash flow. Your business can then grow faster. Seller financing for ten years or more is not unusual.

Third, sellers finance more of the price. Sellers know what their business is worth and are less cautious than banks because if you default, the seller can take back his business. A bank or another lender must liquidate the business. So sellers can be more lenient on how much of the price they will finance.

Fourth, sellers may not demand outside personal collateral because the seller has the best collateral – his own business. Sellers have less leverage than banks to demand additional collateral. Usually you will only personally guarantee the loan, and give the seller a mortgage on the business.

Finally, sellers can be more forgiving. Sellers understand their business. If business is slow, and you miss a payment or two, a seller may be more forgiving than a bank.

Are SBA loans easier to get credit-wise?

The Small Business Administration (SBA) mission is to 'help people get into business and stay in business.' They guarantee loans made by banks to small businesses; 'independently owned and operated, and not dominant in their field.' This doesn't mean you must remain a small business, but only be a small business when you apply for an SBA loan.

The SBA rarely makes direct loans, unless your business serves a depressed area. Typically, SBA's loans are made by a local bank. The SBA guarantees 90 percent of the loan. Because the loan is guaranteed, these banks can resell their loan. Few direct SBA loans are approved. To qualify for an SBA guaranteed loan, you must prove that you were rejected by two private lenders. So inevitably the poorer credit risks wins approval.

There are also disadvantages to SBA loans. For example, the SBA will want extensive personal collateral (a mortgage on your home). The SBA can take up to six months to process a loan. Finally, the SBA will expect you to match revenues so you may need to invest about one-half of the purchase price. As with banks, the SBA discourages secondary financing or high-leverage deals.

Will my poor credit affect my chances of getting a student loan?

Bad credit generally is not a valid reason for lenders to refuse to grant a student loan. One exception is when parents apply for PLUS loans.

How much debt do consumers owe?

The figure is now over $2.5 trillion as of June 2008. That's a 6.34 percent increase over the prior year. Much of this is credit card debt.

FIVE

HOW TO PROTECT YOUR CREDIT

It's not enough to develop good credit. You also have to know how to maintain your great credit. This requires sound financial planning. The essence of good financial planning is to know how to budget, identify budget problems, how to use and revise budgets, and how to avoid those inevitable problems that destroy credit: Non-payments, late payments, bankruptcy, foreclosure, repossession and tax liens.

How can I avoid future credit and financial problems? It seems that I am constantly in debt.

We each have our own reasons for our financial problems, so there is no one answer. However, there are some basic rules to good money management, and if your follow them you can greatly improve your finances and improve the odds that you will stay out of trouble.

1. *Set a realistic budget and stick with it.* A budget is your blueprint for spending and an essential first step.

2. *Avoid sales and impulse buying.* Buy only what you absolutely need. And don't buy only because something's on sale. Unless you badly need the item, you are only wasting money.

3. *Cancel those credit cards you don't need.* And try to less frequently use those you keep. Also, don't use credit cards for purchases under $10.

4. *Avoid large house payments, expensive rents or big car payments.* If your housing and transportation expenses consume more than one-third of your net income, you are guaranteed to strain your budget.

5. *Get good medical insurance.* Uninsured health care costs are a major reason for financial difficulty in America today.

6. *Don't cosign obligations* or allow others to sign on your credit card. If they don't pay, it is your responsibility.

How should I prepare my budget?

To prepare your budget you must understand the difference between a debt and an expense. A debt is any bill that you owe that can be permanently paid. Examples are car payments, credit cards, boat loans, dentist bills and club fees. Conversely, rent, gas, electricity, phone bill, car insurance and groceries are on-going expenses.

List every debt. Include the monthly payment, the balance and the projected payoff date. A well prepared budget starts your financial plan. Whether you prepare a weekly, monthly or yearly budget, you must estimate your income and match it against your expenses within that same period. A budget is critical to financial stability because your budget tells you how much you can afford to spend on various expenses. Because your budget measures how your actual expenses match your planned expenses, the budget is also a guide to future spending to insure you can promptly pay your bills and maintain your good credit.

As a compulsive spender always mired in debt, how can I break my spending habit?

Habitual over spenders need behavior modification, as one would seek for excessive drinking or gambling. Nor is it wise to repair your credit only to have it destroyed again and again by constant overspending.

One good solution may be to join Debtors Anonymous. They hold meetings nationwide. Visit their website at *www.debtorsanonymous.org.*

How do I prepare a budget?

Collect your paycheck stubs, tax returns, credit card bills, check books and other financial records to assemble an accurate picture of where you stand today and to prepare your budget. To more clearly set your future expenditures, review your historical monthly expenditures. Limit your expenses to what you presently spend. Do not, for now, include your debts. If your income and expenses vary from month-to-month, prepare separate monthly budgets. Then compare your monthly income and expenses. The difference will be either a surplus or deficit which will allow you to revise your budget accordingly.

How do I set a budget period?

Most families use an annual budget, but you need not start your budget in January. You can begin any month during the year. If this is your first budget, try a shorter time period.

Divide your income and expenses by your number of pay periods. Most people are paid weekly or bi-weekly. On the

> Most families use an annual budget, but you need not start your budget in January. You can begin any month during the year. If this is your first budget, try a shorter time period.

other hand, they pay most bills monthly and they are not all due at the same time each month. So match the due date of your bills and your paychecks, and allocate your paychecks to those future expenses.

If I constantly overspend, how can I balance my budget?

Compare your income with your expenses within the budget period. Do you have money left for emergencies? Do your expenses exceed your income? Review your plan again. What expenses can you eliminate? Where do you overspend? What outlays are most important and which can wait. Check for unnecessary expenses. For example, can you cancel book club memberships, magazine subscriptions or country club memberships? Must you dine out every weekend? Can you survive without a house cleaning service, a vacation this year, or cable television? You see the point. Discipline yourself.

Once you trim every possible expense, then reduce your fixed expenses. If rent consumes too much of your budget, move to more affordable housing, or extend your mortgage. Or drive a car that you can more easily afford.

If you have made every possible expense reduction and your expenses still exceed your income, then you must somehow increase your income. Is it time for a higher-paying job? A second job? Can your spouse work? Can your children earn their own spending money?

Perhaps your income exceeds your expenses. Congratulations! But don't go out and buy something with that extra cash. Increase your savings to cover emergencies and to build greater financial stability.

Good budgeting requires objectivity, analysis and discipline. Only with a well-defined budget can you control your expenses and set your correct spending level. Because a budget is determined by your current finances, it must be flexible and responsive to change. For instance, you may lose or change jobs or face an unexpected emergency. Each significant financial event will force you to review and adjust your budget. In any event, you will need to review and revise your budget at least annually.

A good goal is to limit your expenditures to 90 percent of your take-home pay. Use the remaining 10 percent to pay down your debts or for reserves.

Have your family participate in the budgeting process. Each family member must be accountable for their own spending. Only through frequent family meetings can you collectively decide what expenses are really necessary, versus those that are only desirable. Then narrow those expenses that have priority and that you can afford. Is it a family vacation? New car? New furniture? With shared family goals, it is much easier to forego that expensive dinner or new dress because everyone in the family knows and agrees upon the priorities.

Make one family member responsible for the family's financial planning. Two-income families oftentimes encounter problems when neither spouse assumes responsibility for the family's finances. Finally, keep accurate records – especially within the first year when you are experimenting with a workable budget.

Should I use my savings to pay down my small credit card balances?

If your savings cover more than three (preferably six) month's living expenses, then pay down your smaller credit cards. But never completely deplete your savings. Maintain at least three-month's living expenses in savings for emergencies. When you consider the small amount of interest that you will lose on your savings account versus the far higher interest you pay on your credit cards, you can see why it's usually sensible to pay down those high interest credit cards as quickly as possible.

I am deeply in credit card debt. Should I file bankruptcy?

No matter how deeply you are in debt, there are oftentimes alternatives to bankruptcy. Too many people mistakenly see bankruptcy as the only way to escape their excessive debt, but bankruptcy may be their wrong solution.

Even when you have onerous credit card (or other) debts, you may avoid bankruptcy. For instance, can you get a consolidation loan, negotiate installments, or even settle your debts for a fraction-on-the-dollar?

You may attempt any of these debt-reducing strategies or combine them. Which is your best alternative? First, check your borrowing power. What cash do you have available and what can you reasonably borrow? If this amount can significantly reduce your debt, then a debt consolidation loan may be your answer.

Next, determine your future earning power. Estimate your net monthly take-home pay and subtract your monthly fixed expenses (rent, gas, car or transportation costs, utilities, groceries, insurance, clothing, child care, child support, telephone, entertainment, etc.) What funds remain available to repay loans, credit cards and other debts? If you have no surplus, consider the other debt reduction options – a debt consolidation or compromise agreement with your creditor.

If through borrowing or applying your surplus income you can fully pay your credit card debts within 2-3 years, then it may be wisest to negotiate with your creditors for extended payments. Only when you cannot pay down your present obligations within about three years should you consider a pennies-on-the-dollar settlement, a wage earners Chapter 13 plan, or a Chapter 7 bankruptcy.

> Only when you cannot pay down your present obligations within about three years should you consider a pennies-on-the-dollar settlement, a wage earners Chapter 13 plan, or a Chapter 7 bankruptcy.

When does it make sense to borrow from relatives or friends to pay down my credit cards and other debts?

Borrowing to pay down your debts stretches your debts so that your monthly payments become more manageable. But this alternative only makes sense if you are certain that borrowing will end your debt problems.

If you are a good loan candidate, where do you turn? Friends and relatives may give you a loan, but before you approach mom and dad or your best friend, consider:

■ Can your friends and relatives really afford to help you financially or do they only scrimp by on their income? Borrowing their money may create more of a hardship on them than they might admit.

- Emotional strings always come with such borrowed money. For example, will your father constantly remind you that you owe him money? Will relationships with your friend become strained?

- Are you certain that the borrowed money will get you out of debt permanently or would it only delay an inevitable bankruptcy?

- Can your parents or friends wait to be repaid until you are financially stable or must you repay them faster than is possible?

Are 'debt consolidation' lenders a good lending source?

It seems that there is an army of lenders who exploit people in financial difficulty. These lenders sometimes use misleading lending tactics, charge exorbitant interest, and collect 'advance fees' for loans they never produce. These lenders advertise 'debt consolidation, debt reorganization, or debt pooling' loans. Aside from exceptionally high interest rates, you must pledge your home, car or other assets as collateral. Of course, it is not unreasonable for a lender to want security considering your financial situation.

Before you borrow, thoroughly review loan terms. Have your lawyer review the fine print so you fully understand your obligations. While borrowing to consolidate your debts can give you a longer payback period and lower your monthly payments, you can expect to pay costly interest.

> Before you borrow, throughly review laon terms. Have your lawyer review the fine print so you fully understand your obligations.

Some lender firms also offer debt negotiation services. They attempt to negotiate settlements with your creditors. Typically, these firms charge up to 35 percent of whatever they save you. Consumer finance and home loan mortgage companies give consumers secured and unsecured loans, but usually want your home as collateral. They routinely charge 15 percent or more interest for second mortgages. Finance companies unsecured loans can reach 25 percent interest.

Borrowing is seemingly the easiest, fastest and most common way to raise cash to pay overdue debts. Second mortgages, home equity loans, or borrowing against a life insurance policy are all possibilities. A home is the most frequently pledged collateral to secure consolidation loans at low interest. If you have owned your home for a number of years, you probably have enough equity to refinance. Refinancing your home will, of course, set you back on your goal toward owning a free and clear home, but borrowing against your home to reduce your monthly payments or even immediately pay down your other obligations, can be a good option if it will put an end to your financial troubles.

When should I get a debt consolidation loan to pay down my credit cards and other outstanding charges?

A debt consolidation loan is only a personal loan to pay your other debts. Finance companies, banks, credit unions, debt con-

> A debt consolidation loan essentially combines your many smaller debts into one larger debt.

solidation loan companies, debt pooling services, non-profit consumer debt services or even friends or relatives are all possible sources.

But once again, consider a debt consolidation loan only if you have serious debt, you can control your future spending, and you are confident the loan will fully resolve your financial troubles.

A debt consolidation loan essentially combines your many smaller debts into one larger debt. Your debt becomes more manage-able because your payments are spread over a longer time period.

A consolidation loan also gives you the convenience of paying only one creditor; as well as a lower monthly payment, lower interest, and a possible alternative to bankruptcy. It can also help save your credit rating. So, why do so many consolidation loans backfire? First, debt consolidation loans probably won't save you money. In fact, the interest on the long-term debt can cause an even greater debt load than before. Moreover, a debt consolidation loan demands self-control. Many debtors abuse their credit again once their debt is paid, and it grows into an ever-increasing spiral of unmanageable finances until no other assets are available to borrow against.

If I do obtain a debt consolidation loan, which debts should I pay first?

Don't consolidate debts that carry an interest rate below the interest rate you will pay for the consolidation loan. For example, if you now pay an annual 9 percent APR on your credit card and would pay 6 percent on your consolidation loan, you effectively decrease your cost by 3 percent by discharging the credit card debt from the debt consolidation loan.

What are my alternatives to a debt consolidation loan?

Sell assets. Borrowing is only one way to raise money. What can you sell? But do be realistic about what you can get for any non-essential assets.

If I am delinquent on my credit cards and other debts, how should I communicate with these creditors?

The first rule: Never ignore your creditors. Creditors won't cooperate with uncooperative customers, so don't ignore past due notices or be indifferent about your overdue accounts. When you have financial troubles, you can't afford to 'bury your head in the sand' and think that your problems will somehow vanish on their own. They won't. And when you ignore your obligations and force your creditors to sue, they will be hostile. So, communicate as soon as possible with your creditors. When you are forthright, your creditors may agree to reduce your payments, extend the time to pay, or make other reasonable adjustments to assist you. Your creditors don't want to lose you as a customer, particularly when you are making that good faith effort to meet your obligations.

Write or call your creditors. Candidly explain your situation and whether your financial problems are due to a temporary job loss or a more permanent problem. Make your case. Tell them what you will do to pay your bills. Will you sell your house? Borrow? Hunt for a new job? Receive benefits soon? And if you will have some money available after you pay your essential expenses, can you send your creditors at least a token payment? Even a small payment shows your good faith.

How do I get with my creditors to either extend my payments or settle for a fraction of what I owe them?

Creditors will negotiate a long-term installment plan once the creditor realizes that your only other option is bankruptcy under which the creditor may recover even less. Your creditors don't want bankruptcy. And if you have a steady income and not overly excessive debt, there may be no need to file bankruptcy. These three negotiating tips can help you settle with creditors for 'pennies-on-the-dollar'.

1. Be honest and up front with your creditors. But do paint a bleak financial picture. Detail your hardships; a job layoff, death in the family, serious medical problem, car repossession, home foreclosure, etc.

2. Offer your creditors your bottom-line settlement – and stick to it. For example, if you owe your dentist $1600 but can pay $600 only over six months, make your settlement offer firm.

3. Bargain with cash. A creditor who may not accept 50 percent of their total bill in installments may accept 30 percent in one lump sum. And this may be your better deal – even if you must borrow the money. Money – not promises – is what turns a creditor's head.

Given enough time, I can pay my outstanding bills. How do installment plans work?

There are essentially three types of installment plans.

1. Self-administered plans (where you negotiate with your creditors directly).

2. Plans administered by a credit counselor. (Creditors are more likely to accept a plan handled through a credit counselor because they know a credit counselor will make every possible effort to help you manage your credit and enforce your payment plan.)

3. A Wage Earner's Plan (or Bankruptcy Court-administered Chapter 13 plan).

How would a self-administered creditor plan work?

With a self-administered creditor plan, you simply send a certified letter along with your budget and plan for repayment to each creditor. Your letter fully explains your financial circumstances and a request for reduced payments – or even a complete moratorium on payments – until your financial situation improves (see sample letters in the Appendix). Your budget should be simple, yet show how you will spend your money. Consider how a creditor will evaluate your budget. They will expect you to make some financial sacrifice and maintain that thrifty lifestyle that shows that you are serious about resolving your debts.

How much should you offer? Subtract your essential living expenses from your monthly income. This difference is what is available to repay your creditors. Divide that amount proportionately between your creditors. Never favor one creditor over another (excepting for mortgages, car loans, taxes, and child support payments which, of course, have priority over general creditor claims).

> How much should you offer? Subtract your essential living expenses from your monthly income. This difference is what is available to repay your creditors.

How do credit counselor administered plans work?

Credit counselors can help you to prepare your budget and negotiate a repayment plan with your creditors. You can choose from three types of credit counselors. Non-profit credit counselors negotiate payment plans with creditors collectively. They do not charge you a fee but are compensated from the creditors (i.e. a donation or 15 percent rebate to cover their overhead). Most creditors agree to their plans since they realize that without the counselor's intervention, they would probably receive less.

So, while it's helpful that most creditors support the non-profit credit counselors, here's a word of caution: These firms encourage full repayment of your debts, and in some circumstances, this is unreasonable. Bear in mind that non-profit credit counselors owe allegiance to the creditors who pay them.

If you can afford their fees, a for-profit bill paying service may give you more objective advice. They will try to get your past due payments current, help you adopt a workable budget, and see to it that your future bills are paid timely. The 'for-profit' services can also help you to maintain your credit rating.

But do avoid the 'pro-raters' or 'debt-poolers' whose fee is based on a percentage of your income. Their repayment plans are less frequently approved by creditors (and after they deduct their fees, there may be too little money left for your creditors).

Who is the largest credit/debt counseling service?

Consumer Credit Counseling Service (CCCS) is the largest (and oldest) with 1,200 offices nationwide (visit *www.nfcc.org*). In actuality, they are independent agencies operating under the CCCS banner, and all are affiliated with the National Foundation for Consumer Credit (NFCC). I recommend this firm for those who need basic services at a nominal monthly cost.

For more comprehensive services, (or if you have been turned down by the CCCS – or other credit/debt agencies), then MyVesta (formerly Debt Counselors of America) may be your answer. MyVesta also offers a broader range of financial services (visit *www.myvesta.org*).

How do I find a non-profit credit counseling service in my area?

You have a number of sources. Contact:

- The National Foundation for Consumer Credit, 1819 H Street, Washington, DC 20006. Phone: 1-800-388-2227

- Your Yellow Pages or Yellow Book (under Consumer Credit Counselors).

- Family Service America, 11700 W. Lake Park Drive, Milwaukee, WI 53224.

- Your bank, credit union, department store or legal aid society.

- A bankruptcy attorney.

How do credit and debt counseling agencies work?

Understand that most credit and debt counseling agencies are paid by creditor groups; the credit card issuers, banks, merchants, etc. So their purpose is to recover as much as possible for these creditor clients.

These agencies primarily structure long-term payout plans with the various creditors, based upon your net disposable income. You make one payment monthly to the agency who pro-rates the payments to your creditors. The creditors rebate the agency a small percentage of each monthly payment to compensate them for their services.

Their scope of available services can differ. Some limit their services to credit card debt while others offer complete debt/credit management and financial planning services.

146 · GREAT CREDIT GUARANTEED

146 · GREAT CREDIT GUARANTEED

What is important to remember is that these agencies work primarily for the creditors. Therefore, their program may or may not be your best option, and you may want advice from a professional advisor who will provide solutions with only your best interests in mind.

What is a Wage Earner Plan and how does it work?

Before you consider a Wage Earner Plan (Chapter 13 Bankruptcy), or any other type bankruptcy, first exhaust your other options. Make bankruptcy your last resort. But, if you do choose bankruptcy, the Wage Earner's Plan will do least harm to your credit.

The Wage Earner's Plan (or Chapter 13) is a form of bankruptcy where you repay your debts to the extent that you have assets and income, over a five-year period. Under the Wage Earner's Plan the court approves your plan to pay your debts. A trustee administers your case. Payments are deducted from your paycheck, which the trustee then disperses to your creditors monthly. If you do not make your payments on time, your case can be dismissed. Creditors also can have the court increase your payments if your financial situation improves. Of course, before you file any type bankruptcy, you should consult a good bankruptcy attorney.

> The Wage Earner's Plan (or Chapter 13) is a form of bankruptcy where you repay your debts to the extent that you have assets and income, over a five-year period..

The benefits of a Wage-Earners Plan are:

1. It protects you from foreclosure, repossession and eviction.

2. Your credit report will not reflect later 'negative marks' from not paying your debts. (Only the Chapter 13 bankruptcy is reported.)

3. You stop harassing calls from creditors and collection agencies.

4. Your debts are automatically frozen and creditors cannot add more interest or late charges to your account.

5. Your creditors cannot garnish your wages.

6. You can later re-establish your credit.

7. You keep your property.

Because I lost my job, I am several months in arrears on my house mortgage and also the mortgage on my vacation home. What are my alternatives to foreclosure?

Foreclosure can be a credit killer. The good news is that banks and other lenders hesitate to foreclose because it is time consuming, expensive and the property may not fully cover your outstanding loan. So most lenders will work with you, if you are realistic and cooperative.

When you cannot pay a mortgage on time, contact and negotiate with your lender (before the foreclosure begins) with twelve possible solutions:

1. *Sell your house*. If you cannot afford your house, then sell it as quickly as possible to pay the mortgage. A sale is preferable to foreclosure because it avoids a negative entry on your credit report and you will save attorney's fees. Most importantly, it will preserve your equity or reduce your deficiency on the loan because you will get a higher price through a voluntary sale, rather than at auction.

2. *Make the lender your partner*. If you can't afford to pay the mortgage, perhaps your lender will accept part ownership

of the equity in the property, and in return, cancel part of the loan. This can be a good solution if the property is rapidly appreciating.

3. *Equity-share with a third-party.* If the lender won't trade part of the loan for an interest in the property, that same deal may attract someone who will pay down the mortgage.

4. *Offer additional collateral.* This can persuade a lender to cooperate when the loan balance is close to what the property is worth, and the lender may not fully recover the loan through a forced sale. Additional collateral will make the lender more secure, and hopefully more lenient.

5. *Refinance.* If you have a short-term or high interest loan, then refinance. It can substantially reduce your monthly mortgage payment. How much less would your new mortgage payments be with a lower interest, longer-term loan?

6. *Get a second mortgage.* If you have enough equity in your property, a second mortgage may be your answer. With a second mortgage, you can pay arrears on the first mortgage. However, this is only a short-term solution unless you can afford to pay both mortgages.

7. *Borrow against other assets.* If you can't get a second mortgage, can you borrow against other assets to bring your mortgage current? Again, this requires you to pay an additional loan.

8. *Offer interest only* as a temporary solution. Some lenders will accept interest only if your problem is temporary. Postponing principal payments may reduce your mortgage payment considerably.

9. *Offer a bonus.* If your lender won't accept a short-term, interest-only arrangement, then offer a few 'points' as an attractive bonus for a temporary moratorium. This works particularly well when the interest rate on the loan is lower than the prevailing rates.

10. *Negotiate a 'hold' on payments.* A lender who believes there is adequate equity in your property, may agree to a short-term moratorium on all payments, (both interest and principal).

11. *Recruit a cosigner.* A lender who questions the collateral value of your property may be more lenient if you can add a creditworthy cosigner on the loan.

12. *Consider a Wage Earner's Plan*/Chapter 13. When all else fails, a Wage Earner's Plan (Chapter 13) will prevent foreclosure. Though you must stay current on your future mortgage payments, if your property is 'over financed,' the Wage Earner's Plan can reduce the loan balance to the actual value of the property.

I am three months delinquent on my car loan. Will the strategies to stop foreclosure work as well to stop repossession?

When you default on your car loan, the lender can repossess and sell your car. Thus, you have about the same possibilities as with a home mortgage default. Refinancing is a popular option with delinquent auto loans. If you can pay a 'lower' monthly payment, then refinance. As with other lenders; your bank or finance company doesn't want your car. Communicate. Show how you will make good on the loan. They will then less quickly repossess your car.

As with most purchases, auto sales are fueled by easy credit. Credit problems occur because people can too easily finance cars they cannot afford. This forces banks and finance companies to apply aggressive collection procedures to auto loans.

The same strategies that you can use to avoid real estate foreclosures can generally suc-ceed in preventing repossession of an auto, boat or other person-al property because both lender groups are in a similar posi-tion. A lender who seizes your car must sell it in a 'commercially reasonable manner' and apply the sale proceeds to the outstanding debt, costs of repossession, and attorney's fees. Any balance will be returned to you, and you would remain liable for any deficiency.

> The same strategies that you can use to avoid real estate foreclosures can generally succeed in preventing repossession of an auto, boat or other personal property because both lender groups are in a similar position.

How do lawsuit judgments get on my credit file?

If you are sued and lose, the court will award the creditor a 'judgment' against you. Since it is public record, credit bureaus and other interested parties can obtain this information.

A judgment against you and entered into the public records can remain on your credit report for seven years. Once a creditor wins a judgment against you, your financial affairs are open to the creditors, and your judgment creditor will want to know what assets you own, so they can be attached or seized to satisfy the judgment.

How should I protect my credit in the event my spouse and I divorce?

Begin by removing your name from any joint accounts that you may share. Then directly notify each creditor of your divorce – or separation – and advise the creditor that you shall no longer be responsible for any future indebtedness incurred by your spouse. It may also be worthwhile to publish in the newspaper legal notices that you disclaim liability for further obligations incurred by your spouse.

When should I consider bankruptcy?

Bankruptcy is an option of last resort; and it is only a wise option in three circumstances:

- When you have more debt (credit card, etc.) than you can reasonably pay off within three to five years.

- When you are about to lose your home, car or other assets to creditors.

- When your wages have been garnished.

But before you hire a bankruptcy attorney, see a good credit counseling agency. They may have solutions to avoid bankruptcy.

How can I protect my assets if the credit card companies or other creditors sue me on unpaid debts?

There are hundreds of ways to become judgment-proof. You will find the most common strategies in my recent book, *So Sue Me: How to Protect Your Assets from the Lawsuit Explosion*. For example, I will show you how to:

■ Own only assets that are exempt from creditor claims.

■ Title assets to corporations, limited liability companies, limited partnerships or irrevocable trusts for maximum safety.

■ Safely invest in protective offshore entities.

■ 'Equity-strip' or encumber your assets and protect the proceeds.

The possibilities are endless. Of course, you must be guided by an asset protection attorney so that you shield yourself effectively and legally.

Where can I get more information on handling debt?

Here are two more Garrett publications that I wrote:

■ *Turnaround: Revitalizing the Troubled Company.* Do you own a business with financial or credit problems? Then get this info-packed book. It is essential reading.

■ *How to Settle with the IRS...for Pennies-on-the-Dollar.* If you owe the IRS you definitely want this classic. It will show you how to settle for a fraction of what you owe...abate penalties...negotiate installment plans...and otherwise protect yourself from the tax collector. `For more information on these and other Garrett titles, visit *www. garrettpress.com*

SIX

CREDIT CARD SECRETS

For many people, good credit simply means the ability to get one or two credit cards – a Visa or MasterCard – to charge their daily purchases.

But here's a big secret: Nearly anyone can get a credit card – even those who have relatively poor credit or a low income. Yet people follow incorrect procedures, get turned down, and wrongly conclude that they cannot qualify for a Visa or MasterCard.

Many people with good credit histories and high incomes also get turned down for credit cards, while less creditworthy people carry a pocketful of credit cards. How do they do it?

The credit card world can be simple to navigate when you understand its rules. But to the uninformed, it is indeed mysterious.

In this chapter we will separate the myths from the realities and reveal the 'inside' information about credit cards.

What is the maximum number of credit cards that I should have?

You don't need dozens of credit cards. It is the wise use of your credit cards that is important, not the number of cards in your wallet or pocketbook.

Banks closely track their cardholders, and most banks will want to know how many other credit cards you have before they will issue you one of their own. Banks share computerized cardholder information. When

> You don't need dozens of credit cards. It is the wise use of your credit cards that is important, not the number of cards in your wallet or pocketbook.

one bank within a credit card system (Visa, MasterCard) discovers that you have too many cards (each bank sets their own policy on how many cards are 'too many'), they automatically reject your application, regardless of your credit. Banks that offer the same card (Visa, MasterCard) usually disallow repeat cards to a cardholder. Their objective is to limit you to only one card from their interconnected network of cooperating banks. Most people need only one MasterCard, one Visa and one travel and entertainment card (T & E) such as American Express (Amex) or Diners Club. Owning too many cards can only lower your FICO® score.

How are credit card applications processed?

When you apply for a credit card at your local bank, the process is more complex than first appears. While your local bank's name may be on your credit card, the odds are that your card was issued by a different bank.

Interconnected banks reciprocate credit card processing functions. This allows the network to economize with each bank performing a different service. Most credit consumers are unaware of this interbank arrangement. However, when you apply for a bank credit card, there are many functions that must be performed which few banks can do entirely on their own. Each bank then needs the assistance of other banks within the network.

Bank card operations can be complex. They must solicit and accept new applications, obtain credit reports and establish approved accounts. Each credit card must be printed and embossed. Then there is the ongoing administration: Monthly statements, sales brochures, late payment notices and the countless other details necessary to efficiently operate any credit card program.

To simplify this complicated, costly process, most banks act as credit card agents for other banks. Usually it is smaller banks who contract with the larger banks who, in turn, actually administer the card-related services. However, there are many different inter-bank service packages. The largest card processing centers usually handle the accounting, credit checks, mailings, statements, collections and the other administrative details for the smaller banks. The smaller bank pays them a fee; normally a percentage of its annual credit volume.

Both the large and small banks benefit from this relationship. However, many smaller banks now have their own sophisticated computer systems, and independently operate their own credit card processing centers.

Through this bank card system, the smaller bank can 'stay in the credit card game.' The small bank saves the expense of costly administration. Today's inter-bank competition forces both the larger and smaller banks to offer credit cards because they are so important to bank promotion (they are a bank's major advertising tool to attract new customers), and are also an important profit center because of their high interest rates.

Bank networks frequently sub-divide functions within the credit card process. One bank may offer the card, another handle credit checks, a third (or fourth) bank may emboss the cards and issue monthly statements. Some 'chains' are short, others surprisingly long. While some major banks feature lengthy lines of agent banks; others have only three or four agent banks. You cannot obtain another card if you apply to a bank that is connected to the same major bank which has already issued you a card. If you apply for credit cards to twelve banks connected to the same major bank, the major bank will still issue you only one card. Whenever several applications received from the same individual are processed by their central bank, the first application to be accepted becomes the active account. The later applications are automatically cancelled as they enter their centralized computer system. While your credit card will issue only from the one accepting bank, in the process of making multiple applications, you will generate 'excess' inquiries on your credit report which can lower your FICO® score.

What are the different types of credit cards?

There are three types of credit cards and each has its own special uses and credit characteristics.

Bank cards (Visa, MasterCard) are issued only by banks, savings and loans, and credit unions. The bank cards (MasterCard and Visa) give merchants the opportunity to sell on credit. The issuing bank pays the merchant, less a nominal 1 to 4 percent service charge. The advantages to the merchant are that they avoid financing their accounts receivable, and they assume no credit risk or credit and collection costs. They also generate higher (often impulse) sales because their customers can buy on credit.

Each issuing bank sets its own credit policies (fees, credit criteria, credit limits, interest rates, billings, policy, etc.). Visa and MasterCard do not themselves issue cards; they serve only as a clearinghouse for their participating banks who are licensed to use their name. Credit transactions (adjustments, credit disputes and credit losses) are between the customer and the card issuing bank.

The second credit card category includes the travel and entertainment card (American Express, Diner's Club, Carte Blanche). American Express is the largest. Of course, 'T&E' cards are not exclusively intended for travel and entertainment. You can buy virtually any consumer items or service using these cards. American Express, for instance, competes aggressively with bank cards on virtually every type credit purchase, though most vendors prefer to accept bank cards because they charge the vendor a smaller service fee than do the 'T&E' cards.

'T&E' cards charge annual fees from $50 up to several hundred dollars annually (for the prestigious American Express Platinum and Black Card). T&E cards usually require full payment each month, while the bank cards encourage installment payments, which earn them substantial interest. Because there is only one source for each T&E card, they are more difficult to obtain than bank cards. T&E card companies also have stricter policies on late payments and will more quickly revoke credit at the first sign of financial difficulty.

The third category of credit cards is the merchant or 'affinity' credit cards. They are the oldest type of credit card and involve only the merchant and customer. Merchants' cards are chiefly issued by department stores, retail chains, oil companies, airlines, car rental agencies and similar sellers of goods and services. They seldom charge an annual fee, and as with bank cards, may encourage extended payments to spur buying and to earn interest.

Are there differences between bank cards?

Most credit consumers are surprised to discover how many choices they have when they select a bank credit card and how many differences there can be between even Visa and MasterCard. That's why you must examine your options carefully before you select your credit card. Credit cards are not the same. Nor should you think you must choose a nearby bank or open a savings or checking account with a bank to apply for their credit card. There are as many great credit card bargains as there are credit cards to avoid. So you must carefully compare bank card terms before you select your card.

Other than finance costs, what other features should I look for with credit cards?

Aside from finance charges, consider the extent to which the card is accepted, credit line, purchase protection, travelers and buyers assurance programs, personal check cashing, check dispensers, rebate programs, bonus mileage, year-end activity summary, frequent flyer programs and credit card registration options. These ancillary services can be quite valuable.

Which are the most important features to compare?

For most cardholders: 1) Transaction fees, 2) annual membership fees, 3) annual finance charges (APR) and 4) credit limits are the four most important points to evaluate.

What is a transaction fee?

Banks realize that only about half their cardholders fully pay their outstanding balance each month to avoid finance fees. To compensate for this (and to increase their revenue), banks oftentimes impose transaction fees. For example, a major California bank charges 12 cents each time their credit card is used. Cardholders who considered their $10 annual fee a bargain were unaware of their transaction fees. Yet cardholders who frequently used this bank's card found their transaction costs mounted quickly. So check transaction fees. Bank cards without transaction fees are usually far less costly to maintain in the long run than those that do impose transaction fees.

What 'hidden charges' may I encounter with credit cards?

Credit card contracts may omit or mention in fine print many different hidden charges. For example:

- A bank may not charge an annual fee but instead charge a monthly usage fee.

- Watch the grace period. A bank may charge a late fee (up to $20 or more) if payment is late by even one day.

- A pay-off fee may be charged to a cardholder who uses his card only for convenience, and pays his entire balance each month. Other cards charge a fee whenever you exceed your credit limit. Or a bank may require minimum monthly payments to avoid penalty charges.

- Also watch variable rate cards. A bank may tie their APR to the prime rate or T-bill rate. Some cards have tiered rates; the higher the balance, the lower the rate.

- Still another hidden charge is the cash-withdrawal add-on. This is a per transaction withdrawal fee which can be $25 or more, depending on the amount of the cash advance.

How are annual membership fees assessed?

Annual membership fees are big boosters to the banks credit card income. Because many cardholders fully pay their monthly statements to avoid finance charges, banks turn to both annual fees as well as transaction fees to generate profits from their cards. Some banks waive their annual fee provided you keep a minimum balance on account with them. What then is the true value of this offer? Ask yourself: What interest would you earn on the average amount on deposit? A low (or no interest) account is lost income to you – income that you could earn from another bank that pays higher interest. The interest forfeited may well exceed what you would save on a free or low-cost annual membership.

Annual membership fees are, of course, major revenue producers for the T&E cards (Amex, etc.). Through their various prestige brands (Gold, Platinum cards, etc.) they offer a wide range of benefits (travel services, etc.) that not only produce significant revenue to the card issuer, but offer conveniences and savings to the cardholder

How do credit card companies set their finance charges?

Finance charges/annual percentage rates (APR) vary between 7 and 22 percent, although each state sets their own legal limit. For instance, the District of Columbia limits interest rates to 18 percent (and prohibits annual fees).

Many banks don't expressly state their annual percentage rates on their sales literature because their interest rates frequently change (with interest rates generally, as well as the interest charged by their competitors). They won't disclose their interest rate until you sign their credit card agreement. Unfortunately, a new cardholder may not be quick to return a newly issued credit card that carries an excessive interest rate.

Check how the interest rate is calculated. A bank can calculate their interest in different ways:

1. *Average daily balance* – This is calculated by taking the previous billing balance and subtracting payments. The finance charge is calculated on that amount.

2. *Adjusted balance* – This is the least expensive method and calculates the finance charge levied against the remaining balance. Purchases made during one month do not incur interest until the following month.

3. *Previous balance* – Here the finance charge is calculated on the balance at the beginning of the month. Payments are deducted the following month.

The Truth in Lending Act requires every credit card issuer to disclose their method of finance charge as well as their annual true percentage rate (APR). Compare the APR. That is the true interest rate.

My credit card company charges me 15.6 percent interest. Is it possible to negotiate a lower APR, or should I just shop for a new card with a lower APR?

You can and should negotiate lower rates on your credit card. One recent study found that more than half of the consumers who complained to card issuers about their interest rates succeeded in obtaining a rate drop. Frequently, they saved one-third or more.

> One recent study found that more than half of the consumers who complained to card issuers about their interest rates succeeded in obtaining a rate drop.

How do interest rates for credit card cash advances compare to interest rates charged on purchases?

Credit card advances always carry higher interest charges than do interest charges on purchases. The difference may be several points.

How can I determine my credit limit?

You should be informed of your credit limit or credit line when your credit card application is approved. Credit limits also vary considerably between bank cards. You may find that one bank will give you a $1,000 credit limit and another $2,000. Some banks have lenient credit policies, others are more stringent. Banks will consider several factors to set the credit limit. Most important is your FICO® score. Yet other factors influence the decision – their policy, competition, funds availability and the economy. Credit limits are never permanent. You may have your credit limit adjusted upwards (or downwards) depending upon your credit performance and changes to your FICO® score.

My bank card credit line is $5,000 and I have a good payment history. How difficult will it be to increase my credit limit?

More often than not, a credit card issuer will increase (even double or triple) a cardholders credit limit at the customer's request. They impose no charge for this and give the customer a credit limit of a gold or other premium card, while possibly avoiding the extra annual charges associated with these premium cards.

I have inadvertently overextended my credit limit on my credit card. How can this happen?

The most common way to overextend your credit limit is to buy a number of items, each under the floor (the amount where the merchant calls in for credit authorization – usually $50). These purchases will then not be deducted from the credit limit until the end of the billing period.

I receive many different credit card solicitations. Is there a convenient way to compare them?

Design a matrix to list the information found on their literature and credit card applications. (Some information you need may not be contained in the application.) Then compare:

- annual fees;

- transaction fees;

- policy on cash advances;

- restrictions on how you may use the card;

- grace period before finance charges begin;

- APR (finance charges);

- special services;

- collection practices and leniency with borrower 'problems';

- credit limit; and

- minimum monthly payments.

I am inundated with credit card solicitations. Aren't the credit card companies responsible for so much credit abuse?

To some extent, credit card companies are highly competitive and they issue over three billion credit card solicitations each year.

> FICO® scores necessary to get a credit card have consistently dropped since the 1990's. This means that there are many more credit risks with credit cards in their pockets today.

Moreover, FICO® scores necessary to get a credit card have consistently dropped since the 1990's. This means that there are many more credit risks with credit cards in their pockets today.

Why are credit card companies so indiscriminate in extending credit?

The credit card companies see it as a numbers game. They understand there will be a number of defaults, but this will be more than compensated for by their huge profits on the finance charges, membership fees and profits from their many affinity marketing programs.

What 'hidden points' should I watch out for when I choose a credit card offer?

Avoid cards that:

- charge a fee for no activity or too little activity;
- escalate their annual fees;
- offer a low initial APR – which they will quickly increase; and
- offer incentives or rewards (these cards usually feature above average APR).

How do I find banks that issue bank credit cards?

Banks actively compete for new cardholders so you are probably already swamped with applications. Still, a good starting point is to inquire where you now bank. They will tell you whether you are a good candidate for their card. Or your banker may recommend another bank. Lending institutions that offer lower interest rates may have more rigid credit policies. Higher rate banks are usually more credit lenient. Larger national banks more aggressively accept new accounts. But don't overlook the savings and loans or credit unions. They are good credit card sources. Also check with your professional, trade, civic or business association. They may sponsor group or 'affinity' bank cards and as a group member, you may find it easier to obtain their credit card and they may have negotiated a great deal.

How can I find the best credit card deals?

There is no substitute for shopping and point-by-point comparisons. Nor can you be too careful when you read the fine print. You probably won't find the best deals in your mailbox. Check *www.cardtrak.com* or *www.bankrate.com*. Or call Cardtrak at (800)344-7714. Both Cardtrak and Bankrate list preferred credit card deals.

Will my credit rating affect my ability to get credit cards?

Definitely. Apply for credit with a low FICO® score (or negative marks on your credit report) and you only invite rejection. Remove those negative marks before you apply. Increase your FICO® score to at least 720 so you can get the more desirable credit cards at a lower APR. As a poor credit risk you may still get a credit card, but you will pay a higher APR and have a much lower credit limit.

Also, one or more of the three national credit bureaus may have fewer negative reports on you – and give you a higher FICO® score. If this credit bureau is used by your bank, you may succeed in getting a decent credit card even when you have a poor credit report with another bureau. However, large credit issuers generally subscribe to the three credit reporting bureaus, however a small bank card issuer may rely only upon one credit bureau.

Should I apply for several cards simultaneously to improve my chances for a credit card?

No. Compare credit card offers *before* you apply, and only then apply for the one credit card you want and only to those banks where you believe you have a reasonable chance for approval. If you make simultaneous applications for credit cards, you may be turned down only because your credit record has 'too many inquiries.'

Most credit card issuers review credit reports from the three major credit bureaus, and every inquiry will then appear on your future credit report. Too many excess inquiries within a short time can only damage your credit and lower your FICO® score.

Are merchant accounts always reported to the credit bureaus?

Payment histories on merchants' accounts or merchant credit cards are generally less frequently reported to the credit bureaus. However, most credit applications ask about other credit card accounts, and a good payment record on a merchant account can help you to build credit.

How do ATM machines function?

Automated teller machine (ATMs) cards are issued by each bank for use in any ATM. You receive a personal identification number (PIN) with each card. Each card also has a magnetic strip which is activated when you punch in your PIN. Originally designed only as cash dispensing cards, ATM machines now handle deposits and withdrawals, cash advances on charge cards, bank transfers, account inquiries and even bill payments.

Do cardholder limits on liability for the fraudulent use of a credit card also apply to cards issued to businesses?

No. Federal laws limit user liability only to consumers. Cards issued to a business are not similarly protected from credit fraud. While banks usually absolve consumers of any losses from the fraudulent use of credit cards – even months later (most banks even waive the $50 deductible), under Federal law, consumers do have the responsibility to report losses within two days and they may have liability for up to $500 in losses going back 60 days. Any consumer who waits more than two months after reviewing a statement to report fraud may be out of luck. Banks are then under no obligation to reimburse them. Moreover, depending on how fraudsters gain access to your account, banks may not have any liability for your losses on the fraudulent use of debit cards or the 'unauthorized' electronic withdrawals of funds from bank accounts.

What protection do I have if someone fraudulently uses my ATM card?

Although they are very convenient, ATM cards give you less protection than do regular credit cards. For example, you must report a stolen ATM card within two days of the theft to incur a maximum liability of $50. If the theft goes unreported longer, you may be responsible for up to $500 on any loss. Unauthorized withdrawals must also be reported within 60 days of their initial appearance on the bank statement or your liability is unlimited. You could then lose your entire balance on deposit. To secure your ATM account, keep your PIN and ATM card in separate locations.

Do you recommend that I subscribe to credit card registration services that will notify my credit card companies if my credit cards are lost or stolen?

Credit card registration services can protect you from loss of your credit cards with just one phone call. But ask yourself, how often within your lifetime are you likely to lose your credit cards? If you pay $15 annually for this protection, it will ultimately cost you hundreds of dollars to avoid a few toll-free phone calls. And whenever you add or subtract a credit card from your list you must notify the registration service by mail and retain that correspondence. In my view, it is easier and cheaper to keep your own records and notify the credit card companies yourself. Nor should you forget that your maximum liability on any one card is only $50 if your credit card is lost or stolen.

Why shouldn't I accumulate as many credit cards as possible to get the maximum amount of credit?

Some 'credit experts' may advise you to acquire dozens, or even hundreds, of bank cards to build a huge unsecured credit line. Usually they want you to invest in one of their own schemes. For instance, their scheme may be to encourage you to apply for 30 bank cards, each with a credit line of $1,000, for a total $30,000 credit line. To accumulate these 30 cards, you would maintain a zero-balance on each account and not disclose your other credit cards when you apply for each additional card. You would then simultaneously draw down the $30,000 credit line on your credit cards.

There are several obvious problems with this scheme. First, it is fraudulent not to disclose your other credit cards, even those with zero balances. Second, it is unlikely that any legitimate investment will give you the fast return you need to pay your credit cards. And when you default – as you probably will – you will have 30 negative marks against your credit which can lose you credit for years. Credit cards are for convenience, not to finance 'get-rich-quick' schemes.

Does it make sense to consolidate credit card debts on a higher limit card?

It can make sense if you are consolidating to a card with a lower APR. It can also make sense if you are nearly 'maxed-out' on your present cards. For example, it is not the amount of credit card debt that you have outstanding, but your credit card debt compared to your credit line. So, if you have four credit cards maxed-out at $3,000 each, it would be better to consolidate them into one card with a $20,000 credit line.

If your credit card balance is over 50 – 70 percent of your credit card limit, you could lose as much as 80 points on your FICO® score. It's smart to reduce the balances – particularly if you expect to apply for a new mortgage or other major loan.

> If your credit card balance is over 50 – 70 percent of your credit card limit, you could lose as much as 80 points on your FICO® score.

Do you have any general tips when I have a credit card crunch?

Here are the four most useful tips:

- Compile your credit card statements and list their balances, finance charges and minimum payments.

- Negotiate a lower finance charge on each card (tell the card issuer that you have a lower rate offer on a competing card).

- Reduce the balances first on those credit cards that are nearly maxed out. Pay them down to about 50 percent. Then first pay down the cards with the highest finance charges and pay the minimum required amount on the others.

- Don't use your credit cards until their balances are significantly reduced.

I have had previous financial problems, and lost my credit cards. I have since resolved my financial problems and want one or two cards. Which credit cards are easiest to obtain?

First, get credit cards from gasoline companies and department stores. They usually extend credit to any applicant with a FICO® score of 500.

Once you have established a good payment history with one or two merchant cards, apply for a Visa and MasterCard – though you may only get one with a low credit line and higher APR.

How can I best wean my way off my dependency on credit cards?

Get a debit card which limits your credit spending to the amount in your checking account. Then gradually pay down your credit cards with whatever extra cash you have available.

How do I know when I'm in trouble with my credit cards?

You're heading for trouble when you have more credit card debt than you can fully pay off within a few months; or when you cannot make the minimum monthly installments; or when you roll one card over to the next card or use one card to pay another.

What are the most serious mistakes consumers make with their credit cards?

The mishandling of a credit card usually involves a number of small errors. Most commonly is to spend more than you can afford in an era when so much credit is available. You may have been too optimistic about your finances, buoyed by a rising stock market and real estate prices. The credit card companies play into the problem through their massive – and often indiscriminate – credit card solicitations.

I can't get a regular bank credit card because of my bad credit history. Do I have other options to get a bankcard?

If you can't get an unsecured bank credit card, don't give up. Even with poor credit you can

If you can't get an unsecured bank credit card, don't give up. Even with poor credit you can get a secured credit card (or a credit card secured by collateral).

get a secured credit card (or a credit card secured by collateral). Why a secured credit card? Because banks want to extend credit to earn money. But they can earn money only if you repay. By pledging collateral to secure your credit line, the bank knows that they will get repaid. Banks are strict, and loan officers who reject questionable credit applicants are likely to issue a secured card. Or if you have poor credit and qualify only for limited unsecured credit, you can obtain more credit by pledging collateral.

The most popular collateral is a savings account at the bank that issues the card. This account secures the credit line on the credit card, and this amount cannot be used by the cardholder until the card is fully paid or surrendered for an unsecured card. Some banks will hold your deposit in a CD or money market account. For example, a minimum deposit of $500 may secure a credit line for $250. And you will probably be charged an annual fee for the secured card, though the APR on these cards may be lower than on unsecured cards because the credit is backed by collateral. Some banks charge an additional processing fee of about $50, which is usually refundable if the card is not approved. Other collateral that may be acceptable to a bank, include stocks, bonds, an automobile or boat.

How does a debit card differ from a secured credit card?

Debit cards appear like ordinary Visas or MasterCards. Their issuance does not depend on your credit, but instead the bank deducts the charges from your bank account. The debit card thus gives you the convenience of a credit card while allowing you to keep your funds in a higher interest money market account. Debit cards are thus similar to checking accounts. The one difference is that it is often more convenient to use a charge card than to write a check, and while most vendors accept charge cards, far fewer will accept checks.

If you have liquid assets and cannot qualify for an unsecured credit card, then a debit card may be your answer. Debit cards are also available from larger brokerage firms – such as Prudential Bache. You can set up a debit card through their money market accounts.

Because secured bank cards and debit cards are backed by either cash on deposit or collateral, the bank cannot lose. That is why they accept poor credit risks. However, these cards can give you the convenience of a credit card when you cannot obtain an unsecured card. And once you prove your creditworthiness with a secured credit card, you can build the credit necessary to qualify for an unsecured credit card.

What is the significance of becoming an 'authorized user' on a credit card?

Becoming an authorized user is not as good as credit established in your own name. Nevertheless, a favorable credit entry on an account where you are an authorized user will reflect favorably on your credit rating and, similarly, an unfavorable entry will reflect unfavorably on your credit.

If I pay promptly my secured credit cards, will it improve my credit score?

Not necessarily. A good payment record on a secured or debit card is not automatically reported to the credit bureau. You want a secured card from a bank who will report your secured credit card history to the credit bu-

> A good payment record on a secured or debit card is not automatically reported to the credit bureau. You want a secured card from a bank who will report your secured credit card history to the credit bureaus.

reaus. And request that they do. The responsible use of a secured card can be a valuable reference for future use.

Many ads 'guarantee' that they can get you a credit card. What's the story behind these ads?

There are plenty of ads in national magazines and TV that guarantee that they can get you a Visa, MasterCard or some other credit card. In most cases, they are usually promising to get you a secured credit card. They collect a 'non-refundable' processing fee to send you a secured credit card application. Or they may simply send a booklet or instructional sheet that explains 'secured credit cards.' Save yourself their $25 to $50 charge. You can obtain secured credit cards on your own and probably on better terms.

How do I find banks that issue secured credit cards?

Check with your own bank first. Many banks offer secured cards, and your own bank may be most lenient because they already have a banking relationship with you. Request a secured account if you anticipate that you would not meet their credit requirements. Remember, banks do not actively seek applications for secured cards. Also check the credit card departments at a savings and loan. You will find one or more in your area. But you do not need a local bank to get an unsecured credit card. Issuing banks are nationwide, and your transactions can be easily handled by mail.

How do I get a credit card if I have no cash or other collateral for a secured credit card or debit card?

If you cannot get a secured credit card on the strength of your collateral, then you may need to recruit a creditworthy cosigner.

A friend or relative may cosign, or you may pay someone to assume the credit risk. The cosigner guarantees to make good on any credit card obligations you incur, so it is like sharing a card with a cosigner. The cosigner's credit supports yours when your credit alone cannot support credit. Since a cosigner assumes a big responsibility, never ask someone to cosign for you if you can't fulfill your obligations. For example, if you are a student who can't obtain a credit card, will your parents include you on their account until you can qualify for your own?

What is a conversion feature on a credit card?

Once you have established a good payment record on your secured bank card, the lender may offer you an unsecured bank card in place of the secured card. This is a 'conversion feature.' Why would the bank swap a collateralized card for one that is unsecured? Because the bank may earn more money. An unsecured card will give you more credit, so the bank anticipates that you will use it more often and build a higher average monthly balance which earns the bank more interest and transaction fees. Also, an unsecured card may carry a higher APR.

My teenage children are leaving for college and I want them to have a credit card. Should I make them authorized users on my card, or should they apply for their own cards?

Until your children have their own independent income, it is probably wisest to make them authorized users on your card. This will help them to build a credit file that reflects their own good credit history. More importantly, you can monitor your children's credit management and help them develop good credit practices. However, don't add your children on your credit card if your FICO® score is below 720. It will only damage your children's own credit standing.

I have been paying interest only on a few of my credit cards, but I notice that two credit card issuers now require me to pay a small amount each month to reduce my balance. Why is this?

Every bank is increasing their minimum payment requirements to at least partially pay down the outstanding balance each month. The banks are following federal guidelines that now require banks to set their monthly minimum payments to cover interest, fees and a partial reduction of principal.

> Every bank is increasing their minimum payment requirements to at least partially pay down the outstanding balance each month.

Will transferring a balance from an older card to a new card with a lower APR help or hurt my credit?

While you will pay less interest with the new card, you may harm your FICO® score slightly because you will have reduced the average age of your accounts. Another danger with the transfer is that your outstanding balance may come closer to the credit limits on the new card. The best rule: Keep your older accounts.

What happens to my credit card debt once the issuing bank 'charges off' my account?

Your credit card debt will probably be sold by the bank to one of the many firms that buy delinquent or 'uncollectible' debt. They may pay as little as 8 percent of what you owe to buy your debt and they may more readily settle with you for 20-30 cents-on-the-dollar because they will still earn a big profit.

Department stores constantly push me to apply for their credit cards. Are merchant cards a good deal?

Merchants offer many inducements – discounts and special gifts for new charge customers – but there is a disadvantage with merchant cards. Each time you apply for another merchant card it registers as another credit inquiry. Additionally, a new merchant account will lower the average age of your accounts, which will lower your FICO® score.

Is credit card insurance worthwhile?

I seldom recommend credit card insurance which covers your card payments if you become disabled and are unable to pay. The problem is that it's too costly (and also hugely profitable for the card issuers). It's smarter to have sufficient savings to cover this contingency, and maintain affordable credit card payments.

Do you recommend Credit Watch Services?

Absolutely. These services will notify you within 24 hours of any change on any one of the three credit bureau reports. These services cost about $25. Experian has Credit Manager (*www.creditexpert.com*), and TransUnion has True Credit (*www.truecredit.com*).

What should I do if my income is too low to pay my credit cards in full and on time?

Give priority to the credit cards with the highest interest rates. Once these credit cards are fully paid, you can pay those cards with the next highest interest (APR).

Give priority to the credit cards with the highest interest rates. Once these credit cards are fully paid, you can pay those cards with the next highest interest (APR).

Can a credit card issuer increase my interest rate if I have been paying on time?

They can if their credit card agreement has a universal default clause. This provision allows them the right to raise their APR if you are late on any one payment.

What procedures should I follow to close my credit card accounts?

The most important step is to request in writing that the credit card company report to the credit bureaus that your account was 'closed by consumer request.' Otherwise, it may be submitted to the bureaus as 'closed by creditor,' and this will injure your FICO® score.

If I can't fully pay my credit cards, can I negotiate a pennies-on-the-dollar settlement?

You can, possibly, if you are persuasive and persevering. Credit card companies have been known to settle for as little as 10 or 20 percent – but only if you can convince them that you have too little income and assets to pay them and your other creditors. However, settlement policies differ between credit card issuers. Some banks will not compromise the principal but may waive interest and penalties. This is a far more common concession.

If I can't temporarily pay my credit card, can I ask the bank to suspend the card rather than cancel the card?

Yes. And most banks will suspend your credit card for between six months and one year until you pay down what you owe them. This can avoid a negative credit entry and returns the card to you that otherwise would have been cancelled.

How quickly do banks cancel credit cards for non-payment?

Usually a bank will send a reminder notice about 15 days after the first notice of payment. However, they will allow 90-120 days before they actually cancel the card and commence legal action. Banks will also normally phone you at least once about 60 days after the due date.

How common is it for credit card companies to actually sue a cardholder for non-payment?

It's not common, unless the account balance is over $5,000. Litigation is usually not cost-effective because of court costs, attorneys' fees and the time involved. Moreover, many defaulting debtors are unemployed or have few, if any assets, or are potential bankrupts. The oil companies, for example, have virtually no collection mechanism. They absorb their losses rather than engage in what they see as less rewarding collection efforts.

SEVEN

CREDIT SCAMS, SCHEMES AND TRAPS

Those who are most desperate for credit are those most vulnerable to the numerous credit scams and traps – many of which are illegal. Other schemes merely 'stack the deck' so heavily against the borrower, that while they are legal, they are nevertheless unconscionable. Credit scammers prey upon the ignorant and desperate. A few of America's Fortune 500 corporations have been characterized as nothing more than sophisticated loan sharks. Credit is big business, so Madison Avenue and modern technology have convincing ways to get you to sign on to credit 'deals' that may not always be in your best interest. Your only defense: Aggressively question every credit deal and be that educated skeptic!

There are, of course, as many possible credit scams as there are possible ways to lend money or extend credit. While the more elaborate 'stings' are practiced by professional cons; most common credit scams appear more innocent.

Credit rackets flourish because they feed on fear and greed. We each fear that we will be denied something we need, want, or deserve. We also are motivated by greed; the desire to get what we want. These two powerful motivators can blind even the most honest and sensible individual. That explains why tens of thousands of credit-scam complaints are filed annually with the Better Business Bureaus and regulatory agencies.

What is an example of a credit 'rip-off'?

One of the most common are catalogue credit cards from the mail order catalog companies. These credit cards allow you to buy on credit from their company's catalog. Often referred to as 'gold' or 'platinum' cards, they appear to be bank credit cards, but they are not. You may be offered a high credit line without a credit check, and if this sounds too good to be true, it is, only because the merchandise in their fancy catalog is hugely over-priced. You vastly overpay for whatever credit they extend to you. You will make a large down payment (40-50 percent of the price to cover the seller's product cost) so the company loses nothing by extending you credit – even without a credit check – because whatever payment you do later make becomes pure profit. Other credit offers accompany these cards. There may also be expensive application, memberships, or order processing fees. And while these companies may claim there is no interest charge, the 'inter-est' is hidden within their inflated prices.

Catalog companies seldom report to credit bureaus, so you will probably not build credit when you deal with them. They are simply an easy way to buy expensive products through more expensive credit!

TV ads promise to improve my credit by calling a 900 number. How do they work?

900 or 976 numbers are leased from the phone companies by other companies who want to sell you a product or service by phone. When you call these numbers you pay an additional charge above the normal call costs. This charge can exceed 20 dollars per minute! How does this relate to your credit? Because credit repair is what these companies most commonly advertise

to get you to call these highly profitable 900 or 976 phone numbers. They may induce you to call their 900 or 976 number to obtain a secured bank card or catalog credit card, but what you usually get for your money is a credit application and a larger phone bill.

My partner and I want to buy an investment property and we have found a loan broker who promised to get us a loan for an advance fee. Is this legal?

Advance fee loans are illegal in most states, yet there are still hundreds of thousands of people who are victimized annually by this scam. In its simplest form, someone promises to find you a loan in exchange for an advance fee. This person may have the title of a 'loan broker' however, once you pay their advance fee, they may disappear with your money. Legitimate loan brokers collect their fee after they obtain your loan. Their fee is paid from the loan. An advance fee loan broker, in contrast, collects before your loan is obtained.

'Loan brokers' have many sophisticated techniques. For example, you might answer an ad from a firm urging you to call a 976 number for more information or to receive an application. You may be asked to pay their fee by credit card, check or money order. Advance brokers frequently advertise via cable television, radio and flyers. Before you give 'advance' money to a 'loan broker' or 'money finder,' contact the Better Business Bureau, state Consumer Protection Agency or the Federal Trade Commission. Remember, it will be virtually impossible to recover your money if the broker fails to deliver. Be suspicious of anyone who wants you to pay for loan or credit services before they deliver their service.

I have poor credit so I have investigated several credit repair firms. How do I check them out and what is a reasonable fee for their service?

Some bogus credit repair companies promise to fix your credit, often for an exorbitant fee that can cost you thousands of dollars. Credit repair companies can do nothing more than what you can do yourself to repair your credit through patience, persistence and knowledge. And you can do it yourself for far less than it will cost you through one of these over priced credit repair companies. With the information in this book, why incur the expense of an outside credit repair company, whether or not they are reputable?

Dishonest credit repair companies flourish under the banner legitimate financial aid companies, debt counseling services, loan consolidation companies, and credit-fix-it companies. But look for the warning signs when you investigate these companies. Beware of such impossible claims and false promises in the company's advertising, such as: "No credit beyond repair," "Eliminate every negative report – including bankruptcy" or "We can get you unlimited credit now, no matter how poor your credit." Or a company may claim it can get you a major bank card even if you have poor credit or no credit. Or the company may refuse to give you a detailed, written description of its services and policies before you sign their contract.

Most credit repair companies draw their clients from court-reported bankruptcies, telemarketing, direct mail advertising, or even from collection agencies. Some claim to be affiliated with the federal government, but beyond passing laws to protect consumers from unfair credit practices, the federal government is unconnected with the credit repair industry. Others tout "file segregation" as their legal credit repair technique (file segregation is illegally used by some companies to create a separate identity for a client). This federal crime may involve mail or wire fraud and liability for

civil fraud.

Many states regulate credit repair companies. Arkansas, California, Connecticut, Florida, Georgia, Louisiana, Maryland, Massachusetts, Nevada, New York, Oklahoma, Texas, Utah, Virginia and Washington are a few. These and other states require credit repair companies to be bonded (or insure 'up-front' deposits in the event they are sued by clients), abide by the FCRA, inform clients of their legal rights, provide clients with a written contract and allow clients 3 to 5 days to change their mind after they sign a credit-repair contract.

Still other debt consolidation companies and credit repair companies may offer you a high interest loan with large up-front fees, secured by your home as collateral. Or a 'debt counseling service' may be a bankruptcy attorney using this 'front' to attract clients. Other firms offer a national bank card which is only a secured bank card that you can easily obtain yourself without paying a fee to the credit repair firm.

Before you hire any credit repair firm, contact the Federal Trade Commission, Better Business Bureau, state's attorney general or the Department of Consumer Affairs to see whether complaints have been filed, or legal action commenced against

186 · GREAT CREDIT GUARANTEED

the company. And meet personally with a representative of the company. Have the company tell you what it can and cannot do for you and get it in writing. Finally, do not under any circumstances, pay the company in advance.

What are credit card cash advances and cash advance checks?

> Credit card cash advances and cash advance checks are used by some banks to induce you into a high interest loan.

Credit card cash advances and cash advance checks are used by some banks to induce you into a high interest loan. Here's how they work: You try to cash a check at a branch of the bank where you have your account. The teller refuses because it is against bank policy to cash checks from its other branches, so it is suggested that the bank instead give you a cash advance on your bank card. You will pay a huge advance fee to the bank to issue the advance, and also pay interest from the moment you receive the advance because banks eliminate the interest-free period on cash advances. If the bank eliminates the interest free period because of the cash advance, it can also do so for the entire outstanding balance on your card. You might, therefore, pay as much as 300 percent interest, though you fully paid the entire cash advance within 30 days. Some banks also charge you additional interest on any unpaid balance in your credit card account which is called pyramiding.

Cash advance checks work exactly the same way as credit card advances. While they are promoted under different names, you are still using your credit card, the charges will still appear on your monthly credit card statement and it will carry high interest.

How do cash advances compare to overdraft protection?

Overdraft protection can hurt you financially. It is a variation of the cash advance scam. Here's how this scheme works: If you write a check that exceeds your account balance, the bank will honor the check but charge the difference to your credit card. Since you avoid bouncing a check, you avoid a bounced check fee, but you will pay dearly because 'protection' is usually rounded to the nearest 100 dollars. If your overdraft is even 5 cents more, the bank will advance you the full 100 dollars and you will pay every other cost associated with the $100 credit card cash advance.

My bank offered to waive my minimum monthly payment for one month. Should I take advantage of this offer?

"We waived your minimum monthly payment" is another popular credit card promotion, and is particularly popular at times of increased spending, such as Christmas. Although no minimum payment is required for that month, you will continue to accrue interest. If you take advantage of this offer, you will increase your debt. If your debt is already high, and you accept this monthly payment waiver several times a year (sometimes you will receive this offer for six consecutive months), you will seriously increase your debt and make the bank card company considerably wealthier. A minimum payment plan (an average of 18 percent interest with a 2.5 percent minimum payment) will force you to pay $4,230.83 on a $2,000 debt over the 12 years and 9 months it will take you to pay it down. Imagine how much longer it will take – and how much more it will cost you if every one of those 12 years includes months in which you omit the minimum payment.

A similar variation is to walk into a retail store in August to buy a big ticket item as the salesperson explains to you that if you buy the item today, you need not make payment until January. What the salesperson doesn't mention is that January's bill may include finance charges retroactive to August.

Should I buy life insurance to cover my credit line?

Insurance offered by a credit card issuer is usually unnecessary and always overpriced! It is the most expensive insurance you can buy, whether it is life insurance, disability, unemployment, hospital insurance or any other type of coverage. For insurance, see an insurance broker independent of any bank card. Be particularly skeptical about credit insurance. Banks love to sell overpriced credit insurance because the banks get paid if you do die, and, in any event they also collect a share of the hefty premium.

Is it possible to change my social security number if I have been victimized by identity theft?

Social security numbers are a particularly valuable asset in the hands of an identity thief. Victims therefore may want to change their numbers to cut off the thief's further misconduct and also to gain a fresh start with a clean credit history.

It is now possible to change your social security number because of identity theft, but it's a tough task. To begin, you must persuade the government that you really need a new number. And even if you get a new number, your old number won't necessarily be deleted from your accounts. Finally, getting creditors to use the new number can be another long hassle. For these reasons, most experts advise against new social security numbers saying it creates new problems, extra work and explanation to lenders and other institutions.

My bank sent me a non-negotiable check which they say can be instantly converted to a loan by completing and signing. Are these loans advantageous?

Not usually. Banks that send you a non-negotiable check ask you to simply fill out their short application and the bank will send you a check for the stated amount. But beware. This is only another cash advance mail order plan. The bank may tempt you with low minimum monthly payments, but their annual interest (APR) is likely to be the highest possible legal rate. For instance, a $3,000 loan at 1.8 percent interest per month, paid in monthly installments of 2 percent, will require 77 years and 3 months to fully pay. And you will pay $24,734.58 in finance charges. That's an expensive loan.

I expect a large tax refund and want to borrow money as an 'advance tax refund.' Is this a good idea?

An advance tax refund or loan against an anticipated tax refund can only make sense if you have a large tax refund. Why? Because the fee you are charged is computed on an annualized rate as though you borrowed the money for the entire year. However, you may be borrowing the money for only several weeks. For example, if you expect a $1,100 refund and pay a flat fee of $84 you pay an effective annual interest rate of 92 percent. However, if you expect a $3,000 refund, the annualized rate drops to only 12 percent. Calculate the cost on your loan to see whether it makes economic sense.

My home needs repairs and several contractors agreed to finance the costs. Is contractor financing worthwhile considering?

Second mortgage financing is common in the home improvement industry where contractors offer to make home improvements in poor neighborhoods to people who have equity in their homes. They are prime targets. The contractor arranges financing with lenders who provide second mortgages with high interest and loan origination fees. Besides the high financing cost, another problem is that if the owner becomes dissatisfied with the work, the lender, who is independent from the contractor, can nevertheless force the sale of the home to collect their money. And contractors who offer "package loan deals" also usually get a kickback, which further increases your loan costs.

What is 'credit screening'?

Credit screening is a serious and growing credit problem.

Pre-screening is pre-qualification for credit. Here's how it works. Suppose the issuer of a new bank card wants to find people with good credit who also earn at least $50,000 per year. The credit bureau's files can generate this list of potential customers. Or the company can send its own list to the credit bureau, and the credit bureaus can delete non-qualifying names. Your name may be on this list with neither your knowledge nor consent. Companies can then determine your financial profile without actually viewing your actual credit report. The only way you would discover this is to inspect your own credit report. If you see the word 'promotional' or letters 'prm' in the 'inquiries' section, it means your file was pre-screened. However, when a company does send you an unsolicited offer of credit or insurance, they must also give you a toll-free number to call which will remove your name from that creditor's list for up to two years. You can also directly request that the credit bureaus omit your name from their pre-screening lists. This keeps you off their lists indefinitely.

There are other examples of credit pre-screening. For instance, a company may maintain a computerized list of persons who file malpractice suits against doctors and hospitals so medical personnel can screen out potential litigants. Or a company may index patients who don't pay their bills, or hotel guests who damage or steal property, or landlords get 'inside information' about prospective tenants. These services never notify you when your name is submitted to a third-party. Since you are thereby denied your right to question this information, it is illegal and violates the FCRA.

My credit counselor advised me that my credit cards are 'suicide rollovers'. Can you explain this term?

'Suicide rollovers' play on the pressure of mounting debt and are marketed for debt relief: It takes the cash advance from one credit card to repay other credit cards. The more credit cards you own, the more credit cards you can then manipulate. And as you

'Suicide rollovers' play on the pressure of mounting debt and are marketed for debt relief: It takes the cash advance from one credit card to repay other credit cards. The more credit cards you own, the more credit cards you can then manipulate. And as you pyramid your credit cards, you can continue to make minimum payments for a long time.

pyramid your credit cards, you can continue to make minimum payments for a long time. The credit world calls this a 'suicide rollover' because instead of reducing your debt, you get deeper into debt. Some promoters suggest that in the 'good times' you should acquire as many credit cards as possible to prepare yourself for the 'tough times.' This is a dangerous trap, not sound credit management.

I see advertised mortgage reduction kits to lower the interest I pay on my home mortgage. How do they work?

Some mortgage reduction information kits can cost hundreds of dollars, and they are frequently peddled door-to-door. They contain no information that you cannot find elsewhere for free or a few dollars, and most suggest the same technique: Cut your mortgage payments into bi-weekly installments to save interest! The problem? Few banks accept bi-weekly payments. It is true that bi-weekly payments can save you tens of thousands in interest and that option should be explored. Also you should explore finding replacement financing at a lower interest then you now pay.

What is a 'pre-payment penalty' on a loan?

Pre-payment penalties are usually found in the fine print of a loan agreement. It can keep you forever in debt. If you fully pay the loan before the date due, you pay a significant penalty. For example, to pay a 5 percent pre-payment penalty on a $50,000 mortgage would cost $2,500. So negotiate pre-payment penalties out of the contract!

Your loan may also include an 'add-on-interest' clause where interest is added to the total amount of your loan before the lender calculates your monthly payments. The total amount of the loan is then divided by the number of required payments. There is no advantage to discharging the loan early, because the pre-paid interest will not be refunded. So you would not save if you pay early. For example, if you borrow $5,000 and the interest for the term of the loan is $500; your total loan is $5,500, whether you pay in 2 or 20 months.

Also watch for uncapped variable interest rates. A capped variable interest rate is an interest rate that fluctuates with the prime rate, but never rises above a set point. In contrast, an uncapped variable rate may, for example, start at 9 percent, but without a ceiling, can rise to 20 percent or more, as happened in the 1980s. Variable rates are dangerous because they leave you no protection during inflation.

What is a computer generated secondary credit report?

Through data entry and retrieval systems, computers can now search your file by code or file numbers. Computers do not search word-by-word for your file. Rather than search first for your last name, first name, middle initial, current street, state or social security number, codes are instead assigned to the searches. The first two initials or numbers of the target entry is usually sufficient to retrieve your file. These letters and numbers collectively produce your "code." These codes will pull your file and also other files that closely match this code.

For example, if your name is John Henry and your address is 5259 Beaverbrook Road, Boston, MA, 02167 and your social security number is 043-45-6789, your code might appear as JOSM52BERRDAMA63043. But if the computer cannot find a close enough match because too few digits match, it will not pull alternate files and make substitutions. The computer will simply indicate that there is no record of that person. If the computer was instructed to find JOSM5BERRDAMA0? It would come up empty. However, at that point, the request will generate a new file. The new file would be JOSM5BERRDAMA0. This new file would have no credit history.

These reports are frequently generated accidentally. For instance, if you cannot remember your exact social security number and you accidentally omit a number, or perhaps omit a number from your zip code, you may start a secondary file.

You can change the order and number of digits by creating new addresses, using a friend's address, or by using mail drops. The links that most influence the computer's search, however, are name, social security number, address and zip code. The applicant must keep an exact record of these changes when requesting the credit report from the credit bureau. An applicant might give his correct name, but with the new address as the current address and a still different address as the prior address. If this results in a "no report available," then you have confirmed that a secondary file has been created with a new credit history.

To avoid dealing directly with the credit bureaus, one can use a credit application for this purpose. Applying for merchant credit cards, or more easily-obtained credit cards until you receive a 'no record' response, also confirms there is a secondary file. The secondary file then becomes your primary file for credit reporting purposes, and the old file is eventually eliminated through disuse.

What is 'skin shedding'? I understand that it will allow me to get new credit identification by using a new social security number. How does this work, and is it legal?

Skin shedding creates a new credit identity. Two systems are commonly used: One way is to change social security numbers. For instance, one may find the name of a child with a similar birthday or someone who died 10-20 years earlier. By using that child's social security number, you have a new identity. The government issues notices of cancelled social security numbers to credit bureaus when a person dies. However, this system is extremely inefficient because it relies on reporting from funeral homes, benefits paid to survivors, closed bank accounts, and returned mail. Even if you succeed in having the Social Security Administration assign you a new social security number (usually because of a religious objection), the credit bureaus' computers may still link you to your old number. A new social security number will then not give you a new identity.

But keep in mind that fraudulently using someone else's social security number violates the Social Security Act, and the Justice Department will prosecute.

> But keep in mind that fraudulently using someone else's social security number violates the Social Security Act, and the Justice Department will prosecute. The penalty is up to 5 years in prison or a fine of $50,000, or both.

The penalty is up to 5 years in prison or a fine of $50,000, or both.

A second tactic feeds false information. Here one contacts the credit bureau where they have a negative report and advises them that there is incorrect information in the consumer identification section. Perhaps they claim that the name or social security number is incorrect. They then supply new 'correct' information which is actually false. The credit bureau then "corrects" the file. Several weeks later the individual contacts the credit bureau to request a credit report. They then inform the credit bureau that none of the information is correct, and that the report must belong to someone else with the same name. The credit bureau must verify this information. Since the information they will attempt to verify has nothing to do with the applicant, it cannot be verified and the entire credit file is then deleted. Finally, these same individuals wait several more months to again contact the credit bureau using their correct name, social security number, etc. and instruct them to re-correct the information. This returns them to their original credit report which shows a clear credit history. The bureau has inadvertently made their entire original credit report unverifiable, and effectively wiped it clean to produce a new credit history.

There are many other illegal scams to repair credit. Follow only sound, legal credit repair practices to achieve your goals. Don't risk committing a crime.

I purchased merchandise with my credit card. The product was unsatisfactory. What are my rights?

You are not legally obligated to pay for merchandise or services that are not up to the standards you reasonably expected, nor are you obligated to pay for merchandise that is below advertised standards, or merchandise purchased on the basis of false or misleading claims. Nor are you legally obligated to pay for any credit card or mail order purchase for which you did not order the merchandise or did not receive the merchandise you ordered.

You must contest the charge in writing to the credit card issuer within 30 days of receipt of their statement. The credit card issuer will then provide the supplier the opportunity to defend the charge. Ultimately, the credit card issuer decides whether to allow the charge. Of course, you always have the right to sue in court to recover your money.

How big a problem is identity theft?

It is a huge and growing problem. More than one million Americans are victimized annually by identity theft. The number is expected to increase as more personal information becomes computerized. Also, too few law enforcement agencies have the resources to stop the spread of identity theft, although law enforcement is now prioritizing identity theft prevention.

How do thieves steal identities?

It is not difficult. They need only access personal information about you (name, address, social security number, credit card information, etc.). Some common sources of this information include stolen wallets and purses; ordering unauthorized credit reports on you; illegal computer tapping; phony telemarketing schemes; sifting trash; and internet correspondence. Thieves also use the identity search companies who market on the web. They can provide whatever information an identity thief would need.

What happens to my good credit if someone steals my identity?

It can be ruined, or at least seriously damaged. And it can take years to straighten out your credit situation.

Bear in mind that an identity thief can get (and use) credit cards in your name, buy a car, make long distance phone calls and incur a wide variety of debts which would all ultimately reflect on your credit rating.

While creditors and credit bureaus are increasingly sensitive to identity theft cases; nevertheless, it can take considerable time and effort to rectify the credit problems. And for many, identity theft is a nightmare.

What should I do if my identity is stolen?

Most importantly, move as fast as possible to detect the fraudulent use of your identity. If you suspect identity theft, immediately:

- Complete a police report (keep copies to later use with creditors and credit bureaus).

- Close all unnecessary credit card and charge accounts.

- Notify your credit card companies, banks and others where you have charge privileges to stop further credit transactions.

- Notify Equifax (888-766-0008), TransUnion (800-680-7289) and Experian (888-397-3742). Request that your report be flagged with a 'fraud alert'.

■ Call Telecheck (800-710-9898), Equifax (888-766-0008) and National Processing Center (866-226-2864) if your checks were stolen. Of course, you should also contact your bank.

■ Notify the utility companies, drivers' license bureau and post office, if you believe your utilities, licenses or mail is subject to tampering.

What can I do to better protect myself from identity theft?

While it is impossible to completely protect yourself, you can reduce the odds of becoming victimized if you follow a few simple rules:

■ Do not unnecessarily disclose your social security number.

■ Don't throw away credit card slips in public.

■ Carefully review your credit charges.

■ Constantly change your PIN numbers.

■ Avoid giving personal information by phone – and particularly to telemarketers.

■ Do not leave outgoing bill payments in your mailbox for postal pickup.

■ Do not disclose unnecessary information on your web page.

■ Shred all documents containing personal or financial information.

- Monitor your credit report continuously (once a month is recommended). This is by far the most important action you can take.

Can I prevent my personal information from being shared with other companies or organizations?

Yes. And this important step can also reduce identity theft. Most companies and organizations allow you to 'opt out' of allowing your information to be shared. To find out more about your 'opting out' options, contact the FTC.

What is the most convenient way to continuously monitor my credit transactions to detect identity theft early?

Experian offers a valuable service where they will notify you within 24 hours of any unusual credit activity. Contact them for further information. The other national credit bureaus will probably offer a similar service, as do commercial firms who advertise on the web and on T.V. But do check out commercial firms before you entrust to them your own credit information.

Can I buy identity theft insurance?

Several insurance companies sell identity theft protection policies. Some policies are sold separately and others can be purchased as a part of your homeowner's policy. These policies indemnify you only for the actual costs incurred by identity theft.

Where can I find more information about identity theft?

Go to the FTC website *www.ftc.gov*. They have an instructive website. Or check www.llrx.com/features/idtheft.htm. The best source: The non-profit Identity Theft Resource Center at *http://www.idtheftcenter.org/*. (You can e-mail them at *itrc@idtheftcenter.org* for state-by-state resources for victims of identity theft or call 858-693-7935.)

EIGHT

SAMPLE LETTERS AND CORRESPONDENCE

1a.   Request for Credit Report (not based upon credit denial)

1b.   Request for Credit Report (not based upon credit denial)

2a.   Request for Credit Report (based upon credit denial)

2b.   Request for Credit Report (based upon credit denial)

3a.   First Dispute Letter – General

3b.   First Dispute Letter – Late Payments

4.   Second Dispute Letter – Remaining Items

5a.   Follow-Up Letter – Bureau Did Not Respond to Dispute Letter

5b.   Follow-Up Letter – Bureau Did Not Respond to Dispute Letter

5c.   Follow-Up Letter – Bureau Did Not Respond to Dispute Letter

5d.   Follow-Up Letter – Bureau Did Not Respond to Dispute Letter

6a.   Objection to Unauthorized Credit Inquiry – To Creditor

6b.   Objection to Unauthorized Credit Inquiry – To Bureau

6c.   Objection to Unauthorized Credit Inquiry – To Bureau

7a.   Request for Removal of Outdated Information

7b.   Request for Removal of Outdated Information

8.   Request to Remove Bankruptcy Information

9a.   Challenge to Non-Verified Entry

9b.   Challenge to Non-Verified Entry

10.   Request to Remove Checkpoints, Alerts and File Variations

11.   Response to Claim of Frivolous and Irrelevant Protest

12.   Response to Credit Repair Service Protest Rejection

13.   Request for Personal Interview

14a.   Request to Add Positive Information

14b.   Request to Add Positive Information

14c.   Request to Add Positive Information

15.   Request for Husband and Wife File Separation

16.   Request to Merge Husband's and Wife's Accounts

17.   Letter to Creditor Requesting Information Correction

18.   Letter to Creditor Disputing Ex-spouse's Account Entry

19.   Letter to Creditor Requesting Reasons for Credit Denial

20.   Request to Send Creditors Updated Report

21a.   Creditor Settlement Agreement

21b.   Creditor Settlement Agreement

21c.   Creditor Settlement Agreement

22a.   Consumer Statement

22b.   Consumer Statement

22c.   Consumer Statement

23.   Request for Secondary Credit Card

24.   Request for Investigative Report

25.   Complaint to the Federal Trade Commission

26.   Complaint to State Regulatory Agency

27.   Complaint to Better Business Bureau

28.   Complaint to Federal Deposit Insurance Corporation

29.   Complaint to Comptroller of the Currency

30.   Complaint to Federal Reserve System

Sample Letter No. 1a

Request for Credit Report
(not based upon credit denial)

Date:

Name of Credit Bureau
Address of Credit Bureau
City, State, Zip

To Whom It May Concern:

Enclosed please find my check for $_____ to cover the cost of providing me with a copy of my credit report. Please forward my current credit report as soon as possible to the name and address below:

Name:
Present Address:
Previous Address:
Social Security Number:
Date of Birth:
Employer Name:
Employer Address:
Spouse's Name:

Sincerely yours,

Signature

Name

Sample Letter No. 1b

Request for Free Credit Report

Date:

Name of Credit Bureau
Address of Credit Bureau
City, State, Zip

To Whom It May Concern:

Please send me a free copy of my credit report.

Full name:
Social Security number:
Date of birth:
Current address:
Previous address:
Employer:
Employer's address:
Spouse's name:

Yours truly,

Signature

Name

Sample Letter No. 2a

Request for Credit Report
(after credit denial)

Date:

Name of Credit Bureau
Address of Credit Bureau
City, State, Zip

To Whom It May Concern:

Please send me a copy of my credit report as soon as possible.

I have been denied credit within the past thirty days by _____
_____, based upon a credit report from your
company. Enclosed please find a copy of the denial letter.

Name:
Present Address:
Previous Address:
Social Security Number:
Date of Birth:
Employer:
Employer Address:
Spouse's Name:

Your immediate attention to this matter is appreciated.

Very truly yours,

Signature

Name

Sample Letter No. 2b

Request for Credit Report
(after credit denial)

Date:

Name of Credit Bureau
Address of Credit Bureau
City, State, Zip
ATTN: Customer Relations Department

To Whom It May Concern:

Please mail me a free copy of my current credit report. Enclosed please find a copy of my denial letter.

Sincerely,

Signature

Name:
Address:
Social Security Number:
Date of Birth:
Previous Address:
Spouse's Name:
Employer's Name & Address:

Sample Letter No. 3a

First Dispute Letter – General

Date:

Name of Credit Bureau
Address of Credit Bureau
City, State, Zip

To Whom It May Concern:

I request that the following inaccurate items be immediately investigated and removed in order to reflect my true credit history, as these items are incorrect and should not be included on my report. Pursuant to the Fair Credit Reporting Act, please complete the verification within 30 (thirty) days.

Company Name
Account Number
Comments/ Reasons for Dispute

Please send me my updated report as soon as your investigation is completed.

Sincerely,

Signature

Name:
Address:
Social Security Number:
Date of Birth:

Sample Letter No. 3b

First Dispute Letter – Late Payments

Date:

Name of Credit Bureau
Address of Credit Bureau
City, State, Zip

To Whom It May Concern:

My credit report lists late or delinquent payments on the following accounts. These accounts are in error because they were timely paid. Please reinvestigate these accounts and update my credit report to accurately reflect my credit history. Pursuant to the Fair Credit Reporting Act, please complete the verification within 30 (thirty) days.

1.
2.
3.
4.

I would appreciate your sending me an updated copy of my revised credit report as soon as you have completed the investigation.

Sincerely,

Signature

Name:
Address:
Social Security Number:
Date of Birth:

Sample Letter No. 4

Second Dispute Letter – Remaining Items

Date:

Name of Credit Bureau
Address of Credit Bureau
City, State, Zip

To Whom It May Concern:

Thank you for deleting those accounts which previously incorrectly appeared on my credit report. However, I continue to dispute the following items. These accounts are still being reported inaccurately and are damaging to my credit.

In accordance with the Fair Credit Reporting Act Section 1681i, please reinvestigate these items and delete them from my report.

1)
2)
3)

Furthermore, I would appreciate the names of the individuals you contacted for verification, along with their addresses and phone numbers so that I may confirm same.

Sincerely,

Signature

Name
Address
Social Security Number
Date of Birth

Sample Letter No. 5a

Follow-Up Letter – Bureau
Failed to Respond to Dispute Letter

Date:

Name of Credit Bureau
Address of Credit Bureau
City, State, Zip

To Whom It May Concern;

I enclose a copy of a letter that I mailed to you on (date) requesting that you verify the stated alleged debt that is still included on my credit report. The return receipt was signed on (date), (copy enclosed). More than 30 days have expired and I have not yet received proof that you have validated the debt with the creditor. Therefore, in accordance with §.1692e(8) of the Debt Collection Practices Act, which clearly states that any information ". . . known to be false, or should be known to be false . . ." cannot be reported to any credit bureau, I request that you immediately delete this false and misleading information from my credit report.

Please send me a copy of my updated credit report as soon as the above has been completed.

Sincerely,

Signature

Name
Address
Social Security Number
Date of Birth

Sample Letter No. 5b

Follow-Up Letter – Bureau
Failed to Respond to Dispute Letter

Date:

Name of Credit Bureau
Address of Credit Bureau
City, State, Zip

To Whom It May Concern:

On (date of first dispute letter), I requested that you investigate certain items on my credit report that are incorrect or inaccurate. As of today, 30 days have passed without response from you.

The Fair Credit Reporting Act obligates you to respond within 30 (thirty) days. Since the information has not been verified, please delete it from my credit report.

I would appreciate your immediate attention to this matter, and please send me a copy of my updated report.

Sincerely,

Signature

Name
Address
Social Security Number
Date of Birth

Sample Letter No. 5c

Follow-Up Letter – Bureau
Failed to Respond to Dispute Letter

Date:

Name of Credit Bureau
Address of Credit Bureau
City, State, Zip

To Whom It May Concern:
On _____, I sent you a second letter advising you that you had not responded to or investigated disputed or incorrect item(s) on my credit report. Copies of that letter and the original dispute letter are enclosed. This is the third letter sent to you regarding these initial disputes.

The Fair Credit Reporting Act requires your credit bureau to ensure the accuracy of reported information. To date, you have not complied. I therefore demand that you immediately remove the disputed item(s) from my credit report because they are inaccurate and have not been timely verified. Please send me an updated copy of my credit report as soon as this is completed.

If I fail to receive your response within the next 15 days, I reserve my right to file a complaint with the Federal Trade Commission Subcommittee on Banking and Finance and the Attorney General of (the state in which the credit bureau is located); together with such other claims reserved to me by law.

Sincerely,
Signature
Name
Address
Social Security Number
Date of Birth

Sample Letter No. 5d

Follow-Up Letter – Bureau
Failed to Respond to Dispute Letter

Date:

Name of Credit Bureau
Address of Credit Bureau
City, State, Zip

To Whom It May Concern:

On (date) I wrote to your credit bureau concerning inaccurate information on my credit report. You received this letter on (date), as evidenced by the certified mail receipt.

My (date of first letter) letter requested that you to respond to my request within 30 days, as per 15 U.S.C. § 1681i(a)(1)(A). Since I have not received a reply from you within this 30-day period, I assume that the disputed information was either inaccurate or that you were unable to reverify the information. The law now requires you to promptly delete such information from my credit report.

Please respond immediately or I will pursue this matter further under the Fair Credit Reporting Act.

Sincerely,

Signature

Name
Address
Social Security Number
Date of Birth

Sample Letter No. 6a

Objection to Unauthorized Credit Inquiry – To Creditor

Date:

Name of Creditor
Address of Creditor
City, State, Zip

To Whom It May Concern:

I have been informed that your company, on (date of inquiry) requested an unauthorized credit report on me. I never authorized this. Your action constitutes a violation under the Fair Credit Reporting Act and is illegal and injurious to my credit rating.

Please immediately contact the credit bureau to remove this inquiry from my credit report, or I will have no choice but to take legal action.

Please govern yourself accordingly.

Sincerely,

Signature

Name
Address
Social Security Number
Date of Birth

Sample Letter No. 6b

Objection to Unauthorized Credit Inquiry – To Credit Bureau

Date:

Name of Credit Bureau
Address of Credit Bureau
City, State, Zip

To Whom It May Concern:

At your earliest opportunity, please provide me with the names, addresses and phone numbers of your following subscribers:

Subscriber Name	Subscriber No.	Date
1.		
2.		
3.		
4.		

According to my credit report (see attached copy), these subscribers, without authorization, requested credit reports on me. I wish to directly contact them to find out the purpose of such request.

Your immediate attention to this matter is appreciated.

Sincerely,

Signature

Name
Address
Social Security Number
Date of Birth

Sample Letter No. 6c

Objection to Unauthorized
Credit Inquiry – To Credit Bureau

Date:

Name of Credit Bureau
Address of Credit Bureau
City, State, Zip

To Whom It May Concern:

The following inquiries were not authorized by me. Please delete them. The continued presence of these inquiries on my credit report constitutes inaccurate information, which, under the Fair Credit Reporting Act, must be removed.

1.
2.
3.
4.

Furthermore, I would appreciate the names, addresses and phone numbers of these companies so I may contact them directly.

Sincerely,

Signature

Name
Address
Social Security Number
Date of Birth

Sample Letter No. 7a

Request to Remove Outdated Information

Date:

Name of Credit Bureau
Address of Credit Bureau
City, State, Zip

To Whom It May Concern:

Under Section 1681c of the Federal Fair Credit Reporting Act you are obligated to delete obsolete information from my credit report.

Please refer to the information circled on the attached copy of the consumer credit report. These items are obsolete and should be deleted immediately from my credit file.

I anticipate your immediate attention to this matter.

Sincerely,

Signature

Name
Address
Social Security Number
Date of Birth

Sample Letter No. 7b

Request to Remove Outdated Information

Date:

Name of Credit Bureau
Address of Credit Bureau
City, State, Zip

To Whom It May Concern:

I have received my current credit report and bring to your attention several outdated entries.

1.
2.
3.

These entries are more than seven years old and thus exceed the statutory reporting time period under the Fair Credit Reporting Act, and must be removed. Please send my updated/revised credit report to me once these entries have been deleted.

Your prompt attention to this matter is appreciated.

Sincerely,

Signature

Name
Address
Social Security Number
Date of Birth

Sample Letter No. 8

Request to Remove Information on
Non-Adjudicated Bankruptcy

Date:

Name of Credit Bureau
Address of Credit Bureau
City, State, Zip

To Whom It May Concern:

You list a dismissed (filed) bankruptcy as confirmed. Although it may be your policy to report bankruptcies which are filed, dismissed or adjudicated for ten years, the Fair Credit Reporting Act mentions nothing in Section 1681c relating to dismissed or withdrawn bankruptcies. The law clearly states from "date of adjudication" or date of 'order for relief'.

A bankruptcy dismissed no longer exists and a case filed was never adjudicated. Therefore, you cannot maintain this information on my credit report.

Accordingly, under Section 1681(a)(5) of the FCRA you must delete this bankruptcy reference from my credit report and send me an updated copy when it is completed.

Sincerely,

Signature

Name
Address
Social Security Number
Date of Birth

Sample Letter No. 9a

Challenge to Non-Verified Entry

Date:

Name of Credit Bureau
Address of Credit Bureau
City, State, Zip

To Whom It May Concern:

In accordance with the law, I have sent a letter (copy attached) to the following creditors to verify the debts that my credit report alleges that I owe them. Since these creditors cannot verify these debts to me, as the alleged debtor, your credit bureau cannot have verified them.

Since these debts remain unverified according to the law, please remove reference to these accounts from my credit report within the next 30 days.

Sincerely,

Signature

Name
Address
Social Security Number
Date of Birth

Sample Letter No. 9b

Challenge to Non-Verified Entry

Date:

Name of Collection Agency
Address of Collection Agency
City, State, Zip

To Whom It May Concern:

I have received a letter claiming that I owe a debt to (name). This is in error. I request you to send me the following proof as you are obligated to do in accordance with the Debt Collection Practices Act, Section 1692g.

1.   The original application or contract

2.   Any and all statements allegedly related to this debt

3.   Any and all signed receipts

4.   Any and all canceled checks.

Under the law, you have 30 days to supply this verification.

Sincerely,

Signature

Name
Address
Social Security Number
Date of Birth

Sample Letter No. 10

Request to Remove Checkpoints,
Alerts and File Variations

Date:

Name of Credit Bureau
Address of Credit Bureau
City, State, Zip

To Whom It May Concern:
Please remove the following checkpoints, alerts and file variations
which are being maintained incorrectly on my credit report. These
errors on my credit report make it appear as though I engaged in
fraud concerning credit matters.

The only information that should appear on my report is the
corrected information in this letter. Please enter these corrections
and send me a copy of my updated report.

1.
2.
3.

Also, please provide me with the names, addresses and phone
numbers of any companies who caused these errors so I may have
them correct the errors on their records.

Sincerely,

Signature

Name
Address
Social Security Number
Date of Birth

Sample Letter No. 11

*Response to Claim of Frivolous
and Irrelevant Protest*

Date:

Name of Credit Bureau
Address of Credit Bureau
City, State, Zip

To Whom It May Concern:

I am in receipt of your letter dated (date) claiming that my credit dispute is "frivolous and/or irrelevant." You cannot know that because you have not fulfilled your obligation under the law to re-investigate the matter.

I shall forward a copy of your letter to the Federal Trade Commission and to the subcommittee on Banking, Credit and Insurance unless you fulfill your legal obligation and re-investigate the items contained in my letter dated (date) and sent to you certified mail, return receipt requested.

Please confirm when the process is completed.

Sincerely,

Signature

Name
Address
Social Security Number
Date of Birth

Sample Letter No. 12

Response to Credit Repair
Service Protest Rejection

Date:

Name of Credit Bureau
Address of Credit Bureau
City, State, Zip

To Whom It May Concern:

I reply to your illegal letter dated (date), where you state that you have no obligation to investigate disputed entries listed in my letter to you dated (date) sent return receipt requested (copy enclosed), because I use a "credit repair service" to assist me in this matter:

1. The FCRA obligates you to investigate any disputed claim within 30 days. The FCRA does not provide exceptions when credit repair services intervene. So far, you have not fulfilled your obligation to verify and are in clear violation of the law.

Therefore, I expect you to complete the verification process within 30 (thirty) days from your receipt of this letter. If I fail to receive confirmation within that time, I will forward a copy of all correspondence together with a formal complaint to the Federal Trade Commission, in addition to the state consumer protection agencies.

Sincerely,

Signature

Name
Address
Social Security Number
Date of Birth

Sample Letter No. 13

Request for Personal Interview

Date:

Name of Credit Bureau
Address of Credit Bureau
City, State, Zip

To Whom It May Concern:

Under Sections 1681h(b)(2)(A) of the Federal Fair Credit Reporting Act, the undersigned is entitled to a personal interview with your credit bureau to obtain a copy of the consumer credit report issued by you and to review my credit files.

Therefore, I will be at your office on (date) at (time) a.m./p.m. If this date or time is inconvenient, please advise so that I may arrange a mutually agreeable date and/or time.

Within the last thirty (30) days, I have received notice of credit denial wholly or partly as a result of a credit report from your bureau.

Please find a copy of the denial letter. Please also have my client files ready for review.

Sincerely,

Signature

Name
Address
Social Security Number
Date of Birth

Sample Letter No. 14a

Request to Add Positive Credit Information

Date:

Name of Credit Bureau
Address of Credit Bureau
City, State, Zip

To Whom It May Concern:

I have reviewed my credit report, and find that you do not list the following credit accounts. Please add this information to my credit report.

If there is any fee for this service, please advise.

> Creditor
> Address
> Type Account
> Account Number
> Date Opened
> Credit Limit
> Balance

Your cooperation in this matter is appreciated.

Sincerely,

Signature

Name
Address
Social Security Number
Date of Birth

Sample Letter No. 14b

Request to Add Positive Information

Date:

Name of Credit Bureau
Address of Credit Bureau
City, State, Zip

To Whom It May Concern:

Please add the following credit references to my credit report.

> Creditor's Name
> Creditor's Address
> Account Number

Please send me an updated credit report as soon as the above accounts have been added. If there is any fee for this, please advise.

Thank you for your assistance in this matter.

Sincerely,

Signature

Name
Address
Social Security Number
Date of Birth

Sample Letter No. 14c

Request to Add Positive Information

Date:

Name of Credit Bureau
Address of Credit Bureau
City, State, Zip

To Whom It May Concern:

In reviewing my credit file, I find that my credit record fails to include information that is important to provide prospective creditors a complete or accurate profile of me as a credit consumer. I therefore request that you add the following information to my credit report:

> Creditor:
> Creditor's Address:
> Account Number:
> Account Type:

Should you need additional information, I can be reached at (area code/telephone number and mailing address). Please let me know if there is a fee for this service.

Thank you for your attention to this matter.

Sincerely,

Signature
Name
Address
Social Security Number
Date of Birth

Sample Letter No. 15

Request for Husband and Wife File Separation

Date:

Name of Creditor
Address of Creditor
City, State, Zip

To Whom It May Concern:
Current Account Number:

Under the Equal Opportunity Act, a husband and wife are allowed to maintain separate credit files.

The undersigned request that credit information on the accounts of the undersigned be maintained separately to the extent required by law.

We further request that all past, current and future credit information be reported separately.

Sincerely,

Husband's Signature
Husband's Name

Wife's Signature
Wife's Name

Address

Sample Letter No. 16

*Request to Combine Husband's
and Wife's Credit Files*

Date:

Name of Creditor
Address of Creditor
City, State, Zip

To Whom It May Concern:

We request all information concerning the accounts listed below
be reported as one account, as provided for by the Equal Credit
Opportunity Act, Regulation B.

      Name:
      Spouse's Name:
      Current Account Name:
      Account Number:

Sincerely,

Signature of Either Spouse

Name
Address

Sample Letter No. 17

Letter to Creditor Requesting Information Correction

Date:

Name of Creditor
Address of Creditor
City, State, Zip

Dear Credit Manager:
I received a copy of my credit report from (name of credit bureau).
Upon reviewing the report, I discovered a problem relating to my
account with you. My account number is _____.

The problem is: (describe the problem clearly and briefly).

Enclosed please find documentation to support my case.

Please investigate this and notify me of your findings. If the
information you have reported to the credit bureaus has not been
accurate and complete, please provide the correct information
to the credit bureaus and direct that they make the appropriate
corrections on my credit files.

In addition, please send me a copy of whatever information you
send the credit bureaus in response to this letter. Please send that
information to me at (mailing address).
I can be reached at (phone number).
Your prompt attention to this request is appreciated.

Sincerely,

Signature

Name
Address
Account Number

Sample Letter No. 18

Letter to Creditor Disputing Ex-spouse's Account Entry

Date:

Name of Creditor
Address of Creditor
City, State, Zip

Re: Account Number

To Whom It May Concern:

I have examined my current credit bureau report and it has come to my attention that your company has mistakenly recorded the payment history/liability for the account referenced above.

This account belongs to my ex-spouse, (name), and is solely his/her responsibility. We have been divorced since (number of years) and I am not responsible for this account.

Under the Fair Credit Reporting Act, you have 30 days from the date of receipt of this letter to remove this information from the records of the credit bureaus you have reported this inaccurate information to.

I anticipate your prompt response.

Sincerely,

Signature

Name
Address
Social Security Number
Date of Birth

Sample Letter No. 19

Letter to Creditor Requesting
Reasons for Credit Denial

Date:

Name of Creditor
Address of Creditor
City, State, Zip

To Whom It May Concern:

I was denied credit by your company.

Under Section 1681m(b) of the Federal Fair Credit Reporting Act, I hereby request full disclosure of the factual information disclosed to you by persons other than Consumer Reporting Agencies concerning the undersigned. This information must be in sufficient detail to allow me to refute, challenge or dispute its accuracy.

Please take further notice that you are required to render such notification to me within thirty (30) days as per the FCRA.

Sincerely,

Signature

Name
Address
City, State, Zip

Sample Letter No. 20

Request to Send Creditors Updated Report

Date:

Name of Credit Bureau
Address of Credit Bureau
City, State, Zip

To Whom It May Concern:

Pursuant to Section 1681i(d) of the Federal Fair Credit Reporting Act, I request that you notify every party who has received the deleted or disputed information within the past two (2) years and notify them that such information has been subsequently deleted.

If there is any fee for this service, please notify me immediately.

Sincerely,

Signature

Name
Address
Social Security Number
Date of Birth

Sample Letter No. 21a

Creditor Settlement Agreement

Date:
Name of Creditor
Address of Creditor
City, State, Zip   Re: Account
Number

Dear :
This letter confirms our telephone conversation on (date) regarding settlement of the above account.

As agreed, I shall pay your company the amount of $_____ to fully settle this account.

Upon receipt of the above payment, you have agreed to change the entry on my credit file to 'paid satisfactory.' In addition, adverse credit information regarding my account, such as 'late payment' or 'charge off' shall be deleted from my report.

If you agree to the aforementioned terms and conditions, please acknowledge same with your signature and return one copy. Upon receipt, I shall immediately forward you a check for the amount stated above.

Signature of Authorized Officer
Date

Name
Title

Sincerely,
Signature
Name
Address

Sample Letter No. 21b

Creditor Settlement Agreement

Date:

Name of Creditor
Address of Creditor
City, State, Zip

Gentlemen:

I write to confirm our agreement regarding settlement of a debt that I owe to your company. The terms I propose are as follows:

1. "I," (your name), agree to pay (creditor's name) ("You") $(dollar amount) in full satisfaction of all amounts that I owe to You and You agree to accept $(dollar amount) from me in full satisfaction of all amounts that I owe to You.

2. I agree to pay the $(dollar amount) in (number) monthly installments of $(dollar amount), without interest. The first payment to begin on (date) and each remaining payment on the (day) of each following month. I will mail these payments to your office, located at (address).

3. If I do not pay the full amount of each payment when it is due, I will be in default. If I am in default, You may send me a written notice telling me that if I do not pay the overdue amount by a certain date, the entire unpaid balance will be due within 30 days after the date on which the notice is delivered or mailed to me.

4. Upon discharging this debt, you agree to notify each credit bureau to which You report credit information that any adverse credit information regarding my account with You is no longer verifiable and should be deleted from my credit report.

If You agree to the foregoing terms and conditions, please sign the Agreement and the enclosed copy in the places provided and return the documents to me.

Date:

Accepted and Agreed

By:_____
Name
Title

Signature
Your Name
Address
Account Number

Sample Letter No. 21c

Request to Add Consumer Statement

Date:

Name of Credit Bureau
Address of Credit Bureau
City, State, Zip

To Whom It May Concern:

I request that you include the following consumer statement in my credit report:

Pursuant to the Fair Credit Reporting Act, Section 1681i(a)(5)(B)(iii)(III), you are obligated to include my statement, or fair summary thereto, in any subsequent consumer report. Furthermore, since my statement contains less than 100 words, I request that you include the full text of this statement in my report, without change, alteration or summary.

Thereafter, please send me a copy of my updated credit report.

Sincerely,

Signature

Name
Address
Social Security Number
Date of Birth

Sample Letter No. 22a

Consumer Statement

Date:
Name of Credit Bureau
Address of Credit Bureau
City, State, Zip

To Whom It May Concern:

Having sent you a letter disputing incorrect information on my credit report regarding one of my creditors and having received notification from you that you would not alter the reported information, I now demand that you include the following consumer statement in my credit report:

Pursuant to the Fair Credit Reporting Act, Section 1681(a) (5)(B)(iii)(III), you are obligated to include my statement in any subsequent consumer report that includes the disputed information. Furthermore, because my statement contains less than 100 words, I demand that you include the full text of the statement in my report, without changes, alterations or summaries.

Please forward me a copy of my updated credit report as soon as the above has been completed.

Please give this matter your immediate attention.

Sincerely,

Signature
Name
Address
Social Security Number
Date of Birth

Sample Letter No. 22b

Consumer Statement

Date:

Name of Credit Bureau
Address of Credit Bureau
City, State, Zip

To Whom It May Concern:

Pursuant to 15 U.S.C. § 1681i(b), I request the following consumer statement be included in my credit report:

Please forward me a copy of my updated credit report as soon as the above has been completed.

Sincerely,

Signature

Name
Address
Social Security Number
Date of Birth

Sample Letter No. 22c

Consumer Statement

Date:

Name of Credit Bureau
Address of Credit Bureau
City, State, Zip

To Whom It May Concern:

I refer to the following inaccurate information presently maintained in your files concerning the undersigned:

> Creditor
> Item
> Amount of alleged debt

Please be advised that the undersigned vigorously disputes the truth of such information and demands the following consumer statement be included in any subsequent credit reports:

The undersigned does not owe the account and disputes the charge for the following reasons:

Pursuant to 15 U.S.C. § 1681i(b) of the Federal Fair Credit Reporting Act, you are obligated to update your records to include a copy of such consumer statement or a clear and accurate summary of such.

Sincerely,

Signature

Name
Address
Social Security Number
Date of Birth

Sample Letter No. 23

Request for Secondary Credit Card

Date:

Name of Bank/Department Store
Credit Card Department
Address of Bank/Department Store
City, State, Zip

To Whom It May Concern:

I, (name of primary cardholder), as primary credit-card holder, request that a secondary card be issued to the following person. I will guarantee the payment on this account.

> Name of Secondary Card Applicant
> Address of Secondary Card Applicant
> Social Security Number of Secondary Card Applicant
> Date of Birth of Secondary Card Applicant

Thank you for your cooperation. Your immediate attention to this matter is greatly appreciated.

Sincerely,

Signature

Name
Address
Account Number

Sample Letter No. 24

Request for Investigative Report

Date:

Name of Creditor
Address of Creditor
City, State, Zip

To Whom It May Concern:

I have been informed that a request for an investigative consumer report concerning me was recently made by your company.

Please be advised that, pursuant to Section 1681d(b) of the Federal Fair Credit Reporting Act which requires a response by you within five (5) days, a request is hereby made by me for a complete and accurate disclosure of the nature and source of the investigation on me.

Sincerely,

Signature

Name
Address

Sample Letter No. 25

Complaint to the Federal Trade Commission

Date:

Federal Trade Commission
6th & Pennsylvania Avenue, NW
Washington, DC 20580

To Whom It May Concern:

I understand that you have enforcement powers against credit bureaus under 15 U.S.C. § 1681s. Therefore, I wish to lodge a complaint with you so that you may be aware of and able to act upon a matter of abuse of that Consumer Reporting Act.

> Name of Credit Bureau
> Address of Credit Bureau

This credit bureau has refused to comply with its obligations under the Fair Credit Reporting Act. The substance of my complaint is as follows:

Please investigate this matter and inform me of the results. The undersigned would be happy to furnish full particulars to you if you need further information for enforcement proceedings.

Sincerely,

Signature

Name
Address

Sample Letter No. 26

Complaint to State Regulatory Agency

Date:

Name of Your State's Agency
Address
City, State, Zip

To Whom It May Concern:

I wish to lodge a complaint with you against the following credit bureau for engaging in illegal and unfair business practices. This credit bureau has refused to comply with its obligations under the Federal Fair Credit Reporting Act.

> Name of Credit Bureau
> Address of Credit Bureau

Your organization is hereby notified of such complaint so that you may be aware of a pattern of abuse and that you may take enforcement proceedings.

The substance of my complaint is as follows:

Please investigate this matter and inform me of the results. For your convenience, I have attached copies of all correspondence. Thank you in advance for your assistance in this matter.

Sincerely,

Signature

Name
Address

Sample Letter No. 27

Complaint to Better Business Bureau

Date:

Better Business Bureau
Address
City, State, Zip

To Whom It May Concern:

I, (your name), hereby lodge a complaint against the following credit reporting bureau:

>   Name of Credit Bureau
>   Address of Credit Bureau

This credit reporting bureau has refused to comply with its obligations under the Federal Fair Credit Reporting Act. The substance of my complaint is as follows:

Your organization is hereby notified of such complaint so that (a) you may be aware of a pattern of abuse, and (b) you may take action to help consumers.

The undersigned would be happy to furnish any additional information you may need.

Sincerely,

Signature

Name
Address

Sample Letter No. 28

Complaint to the Federal Deposit Insurance Corporation

Date:

Federal Deposit Insurance Corporation
Office of Bank Customer Affairs
Washington, DC 20429

Re: Name of Bank
      Address
      City, State Zip
      Account Number (if applicable)

To Whom It May Concern:

I wish to file a formal complaint on the above referenced bank. My complaint is as follows:

I have tried unsuccessfully to resolve the above-described problem directly with (name of bank). The key person I dealt with was (name of bank employee).

I have enclosed photocopies of all pertinent paperwork and correspondence to document my claims.

Sincerely,

Signature

Name
Address

Sample Letter No. 29

Complaint to Comptroller of the Currency

Date:

Comptroller of the Currency
Consumer Affairs Division
Washington, DC 20219

Re: Name of Bank
        Address
        City, State Zip
        Account Number (if applicable)

To Whom It May Concern:

I wish to file a formal complaint on the above referenced bank. My complaint is as follows:

I have tried unsuccessfully to resolve the above-described problem directly with (name of bank). The key person I dealt with was (name of bank employee).

I have enclosed photocopies of all pertinent paperwork and correspondence to document my claims.

Sincerely,

Signature

Name
Address

Sample Letter No. 30

Complaint to Federal Reserve System

Date:

Director, Division of Consumer Affairs
Board of Governor of the Federal Reserve System
Washington, DC 20551

Re: Name of Bank
       Address
       City, State Zip
       Account Number (if applicable)

To Whom It May Concern:

I wish to file a formal complaint on the above referenced bank. My complaint is as follows:

I have tried unsuccessfully to resolve the above-described problem directly with (name of bank). The key person I dealt with was (name of bank employee).

I have enclosed photocopies of all pertinent paperwork and correspondence to document my claims.

Sincerely,

Signature

Name
Address

NINE

The Fair Credit Reporting Act

As a public service, the staff of the Federal Trade Commission (FTC) has prepared the following complete text of the Fair Credit Reporting Act (FCRA), 15 U.S.C. § 1681 et seq. Although staff generally followed the format of the U.S. Code as published by the Government Printing Office, the format of this text does differ in minor ways from the Code (and from West's U.S. Code Annotated). For example, this version uses FCRA section numbers (§§ 601-625) in the headings. (The relevant U.S. Code citation is included with each section heading and each reference to the FCRA in the text.)

This version of the FCRA is complete as of January 7, 2002. It includes the amendments to the FCRA set forth in the Consumer Credit Reporting Reform Act of 1996 (Public Law 104-208, the Omnibus Consolidated Appropriations Act for Fiscal Year 1997, Title II, Subtitle D, Chapter 1), Section 311 of the Intelligence Authorization for Fiscal Year 1998 (Public Law 105-107), the Consumer Reporting Employment Clarification Act of 1998 (Public Law 105-347), Section 506 of the Gramm-Leach-Bliley Act (Public Law 106-102), and Sections 358(g) and 505(c) of the Uniting and Strengthening America by Providing Appropriate Tools Required to Intercept and Obstruct Terrorism Act of 2001 (USA PATRIOT Act) (Public Law 107-56).

TABLE OF CONTENTS

§ 601   Short title

§ 602   Congressional findings and statement of purpose

§ 603   Definitions; rules of construction

§ 604   Permissible purposes of consumer reports

§ 605   Requirements relating to information contained
in consumer reports

§ 606   Disclosure of investigative consumer reports

§ 607   Compliance procedures

§ 608   Disclosures to governmental agencies

§ 609   Disclosures to consumers

§ 610   Conditions and form of disclosure to consumers

§ 611   Procedure in case of disputed accuracy

§ 612   Charges for certain disclosures

§ 613   Public record information for employment purposes

§ 614   Restrictions on investigative consumer reports

§ 615   Requirements on users of consumer reports

§ 616   Civil liability for willful noncompliance

§ 617   Civil liability for negligent noncompliance

§ 618   Jurisdiction of courts; limitation of actions

§ 619   Obtaining information under false pretenses

§ 620   Unauthorized disclosures by officers or employees

§ 621   Administrative enforcement

§ 622   Information on overdue child support obligations

§ 623   Responsibilities of furnishers of information to
consumer reporting agencies

§ 624   Relation to State laws

§ 625   Disclosures to FBI for counterintelligence purposes

§ 626   Disclosures to governmental agencies for
counterterrorism purposes

§ 601. Short title

This title may be cited as the Fair Credit Reporting Act.

§ 602. Congressional findings and statement of purpose [15 U.S.C. § 1681]

(a) Accuracy and fairness of credit reporting.

The Congress makes the following findings:

(1) The banking system is dependent upon fair and accurate credit reporting. Inaccurate credit reports directly impair the efficiency of the banking system, and unfair credit reporting methods undermine the public confidence which is essential to the continued functioning of the banking system.

(2) An elaborate mechanism has been developed for investigating and evaluating the credit worthiness, credit standing, credit capacity, character, and general reputation of consumers.

(3) Consumer reporting agencies have assumed a vital role in assembling and evaluating consumer credit and other information on consumers.

(4) There is a need to insure that consumer reporting agencies exercise their grave responsibilities with fairness, impartiality, and a respect for the consumer's right to privacy.

(b) Reasonable procedures. It is the purpose of this title to require that consumer reporting agencies adopt reasonable procedures for meeting the needs of commerce for consumer credit, personnel, insurance, and other information in a manner which is fair and equitable to the consumer, with regard to the confidentiality, accuracy, relevancy, and properutilization of such information in accordance with the requirements of this title.

§ 603. Definitions; rules of construction [15 U.S.C. § 1681a]

(a) Definitions and rules of construction set forth in this section are applicable for the purposes of this title.

(b) The term "person" means any individual, partnership, corporation, trust, estate, cooperative, association, government or governmenta subdivision or agency, or other entity.

(c) The term "consumer" means an individual.

(d) Consumer report.

    (1) In general. The term "consumer report" means any written, oral, or other communication of any information by a consumer reporting agency bearing on a consumer's credit worthiness, credit standing, credit capacity, character, general reputation, personal characteristics, or mode of living which is used or expected to be used or collected in whole or in part for the purpose of serving as a factor in stablishing the consumer's eligibility for:

        (A) credit or insurance to be used primarily for personal, family, or household purposes;

        (B) employment purposes; or

        (C) any other purpose authorized under section 604 [§ 1681b].

    (2) Exclusions. The term "consumer report" does not include

(A) any

    (i)   report containing information solely as to transactions or experiences between the consumer and the person making the report;

    (ii) communication of that information among persons related by common ownership or affiliated by corporate control; or

    (iii) communication of other information among persons related by common ownership or affiliated by corporate control, if it is clearly and conspicuously disclosed to the consumer that the information may be communicated among such persons and the consumer is given the opportunity before the time that the information is initially communicated, to direct that such information not be communicated among such persons;

(B) any authorization or approval of a specific extension of credit directly or indirectly by the issuer of a credit card or similar device;

(C) any report in which a person who has been requested by a third party to make a specific extension of credit directly or indirectly to a consumer conveys his or her decision with respect to such request, if the third party advises the consumer of the name and address of the person to whom the request was made, and such person makes the disclosures to the consumer required under section 615 [§ 1681m]; or

(D) a communication described in subsection (o).

(e) The term "investigative consumer report" means a consumer report or portion thereof in which information on a consumer's character, general reputation, personal characteristics, or mode of living is obtained through personal interviews with neighbors, friends, or associates of the consumer reported on or with others with whom he is acquainted or who may have knowledge concerning any such items of information. However, such information shall not include specific factual information on a consumer's credit record obtained directly from a creditor of the consumer or from a consumer reporting agency when such information was obtained directly from a creditor of the consumer or from the consumer.

(f) The term "consumer reporting agency" means any person which, for monetary fees, dues, or on a cooperative non-profit basis, regularly engages in whole or in part in the practice of assembling or evaluating consumer credit information or other information on consumers for the purpose of furnishing consumer reports to third parties, and which uses any means or facility of interstate commerce for the purpose of preparing or furnishing consumer reports.

(g) The term "file," when used in connection with information on any consumer, means all of the information on that consumer recorded and retained by a consumer reporting agency regardless of how the information is stored.

(h) The term "employment purposes" when used in connection with a consumer report means a report used for the purpose of evaluating a consumer for employment, promotion, reassignment or retention as an employee.

(i) The term "medical information" means information or records obtained, with the consent of the individual to whom it relates, from licensed physicians or medical practitioners, hospitals, clinics, or other medical or medically related facilities.

(j) Definitions relating to child support obligations.

(1) Overdue support. The term "overdue support has the meaning given to such term in section 666(e) of title 42 [Social Security Act, 42 U.S.C. § 666(e)].

(2) State or local child support enforcement agency. The term "State or local child support enforcement agency" means a State or local agency which administers a State or local program for establishing and enforcing child support obligations.

(k) Adverse action.

(1) Actions included. The term "adverse action"

(A) has the same meaning as in section 701(d)(6) of the Equal Credit Opportunity Act; and

(B) means

(i) a denial or cancellation of, an increase in any charge for, or a reduction or other adverse or unfavorable change in the terms of coverage or amount of, any insurance, existing or applied for, in connection with the underwriting of insurance;

(ii) a denial of employment or any other decision for employment purposes that adversely affects any current or prospective employee;

(iii) a denial or cancellation of, an increase in any charge for, or any other adverse or unfavorable change in the terms of, any license or benefit described in section 604(a)(3)(D) [§ 1681b]; and

(iv) an action taken or determination that is

(I) made in connection with an application that was made by, or a transaction that was initiated by, any consumer, or in connection with a review of an account under section 604(a)(3)(F)(ii)[§ 1681b]; and

(II) adverse to the interests of the consumer.

(2) Applicable findings, decisions, commentary, and orders. For purposes of any determination of whether an action is an adverse action under paragraph (1)(A), all appropriate final findings, decisions, commentary, and orders issued under section 701(d)(6) of the Equal Credit Opportunity Act by the Board of Governors of the Federal Reserve System or any court shall apply.

(l) Firm offer of credit or insurance. The term "firm offer of credit or insurance" means any offer of credit or insurance to a consumer that will be honored if the consumer is determined, based on information in a consumer report on the consumer, to meet the specific criteria used to select the consumer for the offer, except that the offer may be further conditioned on one or more of the following:

(1) The consumer being determined, based on information in the consumer's application for the credit or insurance, to meet specific criteria bearing on credit worthiness or insurability, as applicable, that are established

      (A) before selection of the consumer for the offer; and

      (B) for the purpose of determining whether to extend credit or insurance pursuant to the offer.

  (2) Verification

      (A) that the consumer continues to meet the specific criteria used to select the consumer for the offer, by using information in a consumer report on the consumer, information in the consumer's application for the credit or insurance, or other information bearing on the credit worthiness or insurability of the consumer; or

      (B) of the information in the consumer's application for the credit or insurance, to determine that the consumer meets the specific criteria bearing on credit worthiness or insurability.

  (3) The consumer furnishing any collateral that is a requirement for the extension of the credit or insurance that was

      (A) established before selection of the consumer for the offer of credit or insurance; and

      (B) disclosed to the consumer in the offer of credit or insurance.

(m) Credit or insurance transaction that is not initiated by the consumer. The term"credit or insurance transaction that is not initiated by the consumer" does not include the use of a consumer report by a person with which the consumer has an account or insurance policy, for purposes of

  (1) reviewing the account or insurance policy; or

  (2) collecting the account.

(n) State. The term "State" means any State, the
Commonwealth of Puerto Rico, the District of Columbia,
and any territory or possession of the United States.

(o) Excluded communications. A communication is describe in
this subsection if it is a communication

    (1) that, but for subsection (d)(2)(D), would be an
investigative consumer report;

    (2) that is made to a prospective employer for the purpose
of

        (A) procuring an employee for the employer; or

        (B) procuring an opportunity for a natural person to
work for the employer;

    (3) that is made by a person who regularly performs
such procurement;

    (4) that is not used by any person for any purpose other
than a purpose described in subparagraph (A)
or (B) of paragraph (2); and

    (5) with respect to which

        (A) the consumer who is the subject of the communi-
cation

           (i) consents orally or in writing to the nature
and scope of the communication, before the
collection of any information for the purpose
of making the communication;

           (ii) consents orally or in writing to the making of
the communication to a prospective employer
before the making of the communication; and

           (iii) in the case of consent under clause (i) or (ii)
given orally, is provided written confirmation

of that consent by the person making the communication, not later than 3 business days after the receipt of the consent by that person;

(B) the person who makes the communication does not, for the purpose of making the communication, make any inquiry that if made by a prospective employer of the consumer who is the subject of the communication would violate any applicable Federal or State equal employment opportunity law or regulation; and

(C) the person who makes the communication

(i) discloses in writing to the consumer who is the subject of the communication, not late than 5 business days after receiving any request from the consumer for such disclosure, the nature and substance of all information in

the consumer's file at the time of the request, except that the sources of any information that is acquired solely for use in making the communication and is actually used for no other purpose, need not be disclosed other than under appropriate discovery procedures in any court of competent jurisdiction in which an action is brought; and

(ii) notifies the consumer who is the subject of the communication, in writing, of the consumer's right to request the information described in clause (i).

(p) Consumer reporting agency that compiles and maintains files on consumers on a nationwide basis. The term "consumer reporting agency that compiles and maintains files on consumers on a nationwide basis" means a consumer reporting agency that regularly engages in the practice of assembling or evaluating, and maintaining, for the purpose of furnishing consumer reports to third parties bearing on a consumer's credit worthiness, credit standing, or credit capacity, each of the following regarding consumers residing nationwide:

(1) Public record information.

(2) Credit account information from persons who furnish that information regularly and in the ordinary course of business.

§ 604. Permissible purposes of consumer reports [15 U.S.C. § 1681b]

(a) In general. Subject to subsection (c), any consumer reporting agency may furnish a consumer report under the following circumstances and no other:

(1) In response to the order of a court having jurisdiction to issue such an order, or a subpoena issued in connection with proceedings before a Federal grand jury.

(2) In accordance with the written instructions of the consumer to whom it relates.

(3) To a person which it has reason to believe

(A) intends to use the information in connection with a credit transaction involving the consumer on whom the information is to be furnished and involving the extension of credit to, or review or collection of an account of, the consumer; or

(B) intends to use the information for employment purposes; or

(C) intends to use the information in connection with the underwriting of insurance involving the consumer; or

(D) intends to use the information in connection with a determination of the consumer's eligibility for a license or other benefit granted by a governmental instrumentality required by law to consider an applicant's financial responsibility or status; or

(E) intends to use the information, as a potential investor or servicer, or current insurer, in connection with a valuation of, or an assessment of the credit or prepayment risks associated with, an existing credit obligation; or

(F) otherwise has a legitimate business need for the information

  (i) in connection with a business transaction that is initiated by the consumer; or

  (ii) to review an account to determine whether the consumer continues to meet the terms of the account.

(4) In response to a request by the head of a State or local child support enforcement agency (or a State or local government official authorized by the head of such an agency), if the person making the request certifies to the consumer reporting agency that

(A) the consumer report is needed for the purpose of establishing an individual's capacity to make child support payments or determining the appropriate level of such payments;

(B) the paternity of the consumer for the child to which the obligation relates has been established or acknowledged by the consumer in accordance with State laws under which the obligation arises (if required by those laws);

(C) the person has provided at least 10 days' prior notice to the consumer whose report is requested, by certified or registered mail to the last known address of the consumer, that the report will be requested; and

(D) the consumer report will be kept confidential, will be used solely for a purpose described in subparagraph (A), and will not be used in connection with any other civil, administrative, or criminal proceeding, or for any other purpose.

(5) To an agency administering a State plan under Section 454 of the Social Security Act (42 U.S.C. § 654) for use to set an initial or modified child support award.

(b) Conditions for furnishing and using consumer reports for employment purposes.

(1) Certification from user. A consumer reporting agency may furnish a consumer report for employment purposes only if

(A) the person who obtains such report from the agency certifies to the agency that

(i) the person has complied with paragraph (2)

with respect to the consumer report, and the person will comply with paragraph (3) with respect to the consumer report if paragraph (3) becomes applicable; and

(ii) information from the consumer report will not be used in violation of any applicable Federal or State equal employment opportunity law or regulation; and

(B) the consumer reporting agency provides with the report, or has previously provided, a summary of the consumer's rights under this title, as prescribed by the Federal Trade Commission under section 609(c)(3) [§ 1681g].

(2) Disclosure to consumer.

(A) In general. Except as provided in subparagraph (B), a person may not procure a consumer report, or cause a consumer report to be procured, for employment purposes with respect to any consumer, unless —

(i) a clear and conspicuous disclosure has been made in writing to the consumer at any time before the report is procured or caused to be procured, in a document that consists solely of the disclosure, that a consumer report may be obtained for employment purposes; and

(ii) the consumer has authorized in writing (which authorization may be made on the document referred to in clause (i)) the procurement of the report by that person.

(B) Application by mail, telephone, computer, or other similar means. If a consumer described in subparagraph (C) applies for employment by mail, telephone, computer, or other similar means, at any time before a consumer report is procured or caused to be procured in connection with that application —

(i)   the person who procures the consumer report on the consumer for employment purposes shall provide to the consumer, by oral, written, or electronic means, notice that a consumer report may be obtained for employment purposes, and a summary of the consumer's rights under section 615(a)(3); and

(ii) the consumer shall have consented, orally, in writing, or electronically to the procurement of the report by that person.

(C)   Scope. Subparagraph (B) shall apply to a person procuring a consumer report on a consumer in connection with the consumer's application for employment only if —

(i)   the consumer is applying for a position over which the Secretary of Transportation has the power to establish qualifications and maximum hours of service pursuant to the provisions of section 31502 of title 49, or a position subject to safety regulation by a State transportation agency; and

(ii) as of the time at which the person procures writing the report or causes the report to be procured the only interaction between the consumer and the person in connection with that employment application has been by mail, telephone, computer, or other similar means.

(3) Conditions on use for adverse actions.

    (A) In general. Except as provided in subparagraph (B), in using a consumer report for employment purposes, before taking any adverse action based in whole or in part on the report, the person intending to take such adverse action shall provide to the consumer to whom the report relates

        (i) a copy of the report; and

        (ii) a description in writing of the rights of the consumer under this title, as prescribed by the Federal Trade Commission under section 609(c)(3).

    (B) Application by mail, telephone, computer, or other similar means.

        (i) If a consumer described in subparagraph (C) applies for employment by mail, telephone, computer, or other similar means, and if a person who has procured a consumer report on the consumer for employment purposes takes adverse action on the employment application based in whole or in part on the report, then the person must provide to the consumer to whom the report relates, in lieu of the notices required under subparagraph (A) of this section and under section 615(a), within 3 business days of taking such action, an oral, written or electronic notification —

            (I) that adverse action has been taken based in whole or in part on a consumer report received from a consumer reporting agency;

(II) of the name, address and telephone number of the consumer reporting agency that furnished the consumer report (including a toll-free telephone number established by the agency if the agency compiles and maintains files on consumers on a nationwide basis);

(III) that the consumer reporting agency did not make the decision to take the adverse action and is unable to provide to the consumer the specific reasons why the adverse action was taken; and

(IV) that the consumer may, upon providing proper identification, request a free copy of a report and may dispute with the consumer reporting agency the accuracy or completeness of any information in a report.

(ii) If, under clause (B)(i)(IV), the consumer requests a copy of a consumer report from the person who procured the report, then, within 3 business days of receiving the consumer's request, together with proper identification, the person must send or provide to the consumer a copy of a report and a copy of the consumer's rights as prescribed by the Federal Trade Commission under section 609(c)(3).

(C) Scope. Subparagraph (B) shall apply to a person procuring a consumer report on a consumer in connection with the consumer's application for employment only if —

    (i) the consumer is applying for a position over which the Secretary of Transportation has the power to establish qualifications and maximum hours of service pursuant to the provisions of section 31502 of title 49, or a position subject to safety regulation by a State transportation agency; and

    (ii) as of the time at which the person procures the report or causes the report to be procured the only interaction between the consumer and the person in connection with that employment application has been by mail, telephone, computer, or other similar means.

(4) Exception for national security investigations.

    (A) In general. In the case of an agency or department of the United States Government which seeks to obtain and use a consumer report for employment purposes, paragraph (3) shall not apply to any adverse action by such agency or department which is based in part on such consumer report, if the head of such agency or department makes a written finding that —

        (i) the consumer report is relevant to a national security investigation of such agency or department;

        (ii) the investigation is within the jurisdiction of such agency or department;

        (iii) there is reason to believe that compliance with paragraph (3) will —

(I)   endanger the life or physical safety of any person;

(II) result in flight from prosecution;

(III) result in the destruction of, or tampering with, evidence relevant to the investigation;

(IV) result in the intimidation of a potential witness relevant to the investigation;

(V)   result in the compromise of classified information; or

(VI) otherwise seriously jeopardize or unduly delay the investigation or another official proceeding.

(B) Notification of consumer upon conclusion of investigation. Upon the conclusion of a national security investigation described in subparagraph (A), or upon the determination that the exception under subparagraph (A) is no longer required for the reasons set forth in such subparagraph, the official exercising the authority in such subparagraph shall provide to the consumer who is the subject of the consumer report with regard to which such finding was made —

(i)   a copy of such consumer report with any classified information redacted as necessary;

(ii) notice of any adverse action which is based, in part, on the consumer report; and

(iii) the identification with reasonable specificity of the nature of the investigation for which the consumer report was sought.

(C) Delegation by head of agency or department. For purposes of subparagraphs (A) and (B), the head of any agency or department of the United States Government may delegate his or her authorities under this paragraph to an official of such agency or department who has personnel security responsibilities and is a member of the Senior Executive Service or equivalent civilian or military rank.

(D) Report to the congress. Not later than January 31of each year, the head of each agency and department of the United States Government that exercised authority under this paragraph during the preceding year shall submit a report to the Congress on the number of times the department or agencyexercised such authority during the year.

(E) Definitions. For purposes of this paragraph, the following definitions shall apply:

    (i) Classified information. The term `classified information' means information that is protected from unauthorized disclosure under Executive Order No. 12958 or successor orders.

    (ii) National security investigation. The term 'national security investigation' means any official inquiry by an agency or department of the United States Government to determine the eligibility of a consumer to receive access or continued access to classified information or to determine whether classified information has been lost or compromised.

(c) Furnishing reports in connection with credit or insurance transactions that are not initiated by the consumer.

    (1) In general. A consumer reporting agency may furnish a consumer report relating to any consumer pursuant to subparagraph (A) or (C) of subsection (a)(3) in connection with any credit or insurance transaction that is not initiated by the consumer only if (D) the consumer authorizes the agency to provide such report to such person; or (B)

        (i) the transaction consists of a firm offer of credit or insurance;

        (ii) the consumer reporting agency has complied with subsection (e); and

        (iii) there is not in effect an election by the consumer, made in accordance with subsection (e), to have the consumer's name and address excluded from lists of names provided by the agency pursuant to this paragraph.

    (2) Limits on information received under paragraph (1)(B). A person may receive pursuant to paragraph (1)(B) only

      (A) the name and address of a consumer;

      (B) an identifier that is not unique to the consumer and that is used by the person solely for the purpose of verifying the identity of the consumer; and

      (C) other information pertaining to a consumer that does not identify the relationship or experience of the consumer with respect to a particular creditor or other entity.

(3) Information regarding inquiries. Except as provided in section 609(a)(5) [§ 1681g], a consumer reporting agency shall not furnish to any person a record of inquiries in connection with a credit or insurance transaction that is not initiated by a consumer.

(d) Reserved.

(e) Election of consumer to be excluded from lists.

(1) In general. A consumer may elect to have the consumer's name and address excluded from any list provided by a consumer reporting agency under subsection (c)(1)(B) in connection with a credit or insurance transaction that is not initiated by the consumer, by notifying the agency in accordance with paragraph (2) that the consumer does not consent to any use of a consumer report relating to the consumer in connection with any credit or insurance transaction that is not initiated by the consumer.

(2) Manner of notification. A consumer shall notify a consumer reporting agency under paragraph (1)

(A) through the notification system maintained by the agency under paragraph (5); or

(B) by submitting to the agency a signed notice of election form issued by the agency for purposes of this subparagraph.

(3) Response of agency after notification through system

Upon receipt of notification of the election of a consumer under paragraph (1) through the notification system maintained by the agency under paragraph (5), a consumer reporting agency shall

(A) inform the consumer that the election is effective only for the 2-year period following the election if the consumer does not submit to the agency a signed notice of election form issued by the agency for purposes of paragraph (2)(B); and

(B) provide to the consumer a notice of election form, if requested by the consumer, not later than 5 business days after receipt of the notification of the election through the system established under paragraph (5), in the case of a request made at the time the consumer provides notification through the system.

(4) Effectiveness of election. An election of a consumer under paragraph (1)

(A) shall be effective with respect to a consumer reporting agency beginning 5 business days after the date on which the consumer notifies the agency in accordance with paragraph (2);

(B) shall be effective with respect to a consumer reporting agency

(i) subject to subparagraph (C), during the 2-year period beginning 5 business days after the date on which the consumer notifies the agency of the election, in the case of an election for which a consumer notifies the agency only in accordance with paragraph (2)(A); or

(ii) until the consumer notifies the agency under subparagraph (C), in the case of an election or which a consumer notifies the agency in accordance with paragraph (2)(B);

(C) shall not be effective after the date on which the consumer notifies the agency, through the

notification system established by the agency
under paragraph (5), that the election is no
longer effective; and

(D) shall be effective with respect to each affiliate
of the agency.

(5) Notification system.

(A) In general. Each consumer reporting agency that,
under subsection (c)(1)(B), furnishes a consumer
report in connection with a credit or insurance
transaction that is not initiated by a consumer,
shall

(i) establish and maintain a notification system,
including a toll-free telephone number, which
permits any consumer whose consumer report
is maintained by the agency to notify the
agency, with appropriate identification, of the
consumer's election to have the consumer's
name and address excluded from any such
list of names and addresses provided by the
agency for such a transaction; and

(ii) publish by not later than 365 days after the
date of enactment of the Consumer Credit
Reporting Reform Act of 1996, and not less
than annually thereafter, in a publication of
general circulation in the area served by the
agency

(I) a notification that information in consumer
files maintained by the agency may be used
in connection with such transactions; and

(II) the address and toll-free telephone number

for consumers to use to notify the agency
of the consumer's election under clause (I).

(B) Establishment and maintenance as compliance.
Establishment and maintenance of a notification
system (including a toll-free telephone number)
and publication by a consumer reporting agency
on the agency's own behalf and on behalf of any of
its affiliates in accordance with this paragraph
is deemed to be compliance with this paragraph
by each of those affiliates.

(6) Notification system by agencies that operate nationwide. Each consumer reporting agency thatcompiles
and maintains files on consumers on a nationwide
basis shall establish and maintain a notification system
for purposes of paragraph (5) jointly with other such
consumer reporting agencies.

(f) Certain use or obtaining of information prohibited. A
person shall not use or obtain a consumer report for any
purpose unless

(1) the consumer report is obtained for a purpose
for which the consumer report is authorized to be
furnished under this section; and

(2) the purpose is certified in accordance with section 607
[§ 1681e] by a prospective user of the report through
a general or specific certification.

(g) Furnishing reports containing medical information. A
consumer reporting agency shall not furnish for
employment purposes, or in connection with a credit or
insurance transaction, a consumer report that contains

medical information about a consumer, unless the consumer consents to the furnishing of the report.

§ 605. Requirements relating to information contained in consumer reports [15 U.S.C. § 1681c]

(a) Information excluded from consumer reports. Except as authorized under subsection (b) of this section, no consumer reporting agency may make any consumer report containing any of the following items of information:

    (1) Cases under title 11 [United States Code] or under the Bankruptcy Act that, from the date of entry of the order for relief or the date of adjudication, as the case may be, antedate the report by more than 10 years.

    (2) Civil suits, civil judgments, and records of arrest that from date of entry, antedate the report by more than seven years or until the governing statute of limitions has expired, whichever is the longer period.

    (3) Paid tax liens which, from date of payment, antedate the report by more than seven years.

    (4) Accounts placed for collection or charged to profit and loss which antedate the report by more than seven years.(1)

    (5) Any other adverse item of information, other than records of convictions of crimes which antedates the report by more than seven years.

(b) Exempted cases. The provisions of subsection (a) of this section are not applicable in the case of any consumer credit report to be used in connection with

    (1) a credit transaction involving, or which may reasonably

be expected to involve, a principal amount of $150,000 or more;

(2) the underwriting of life insurance involving, or which may reasonably be expected to involve, a face amount of $150,000 or more; or

(3) the employment of any individual at an annual salary which equals, or which may reasonably be expected to equal $75,000, or more.

(c) Running of reporting period.

(1) In general. The 7-year period referred to in paragraphs (4) and (6)(2) of subsection (a) shall begin, with respect to any delinquent account that is placed for collection (internally or by referral to a third party, whichever is earlier), charged to profit and loss, or subjected to any similar action, upon the expiration of the 180-day period beginning on the date of the commencement of the delinquency which immediately preceded the collection activity, charge to profit and loss, or similar action.

(2) Effective date. Paragraph (1) shall apply only to items of information added to the file of a consumer on or after the date that is 455 days after the date of enactment of the Consumer Credit Reporting Reform Act of 1996.

(d) Information required to be disclosed. Any consumer reporting agency that furnishes a consumer report that contains information regarding any case involving the consumer that arises under title 11, United States Code, shall include in the report an identification of the chapter of such title 11 under which such case arises if provided by the source of the information. If any case arising or filed under title 11, United States Code, is withdrawn by the consumer before a final judgment, the consumer reporting agency shall include in the report that such case or filing was withdrawn upon receipt of documentation certifying such withdrawal.

(e) Indication of closure of account by consumer. If a consumer reporting agency is notified pursuant to section 623(a)(4) [§ 1681s-2] that a credit account of a consumer was voluntarily closed by the consumer, the agency shall indicate that fact in any consumer report that includes information related to the account.

(f) Indication of dispute by consumer. If a consumer reporting agency is notified pursuant to section 623(a)(3) [§ 1681s-2] that information regarding a consumer who was furnished to the agency is disputed by the consumer, the agency shall indicate that fact in each consumer report that includes the disputed information.

§ 606. Disclosure of investigative consumer reports [15 U.S.C. § 1681d]

(a) Disclosure of fact of preparation. A person may not procure or cause to be prepared an investigative consumer report on any consumer unless

(1) it is clearly and accurately disclosed to the consumer that an investigative consumer report including information as to his character, general reputation, personal characteristics and mode of living, whichever are applicable, may be made, and such disclosure

(A) is made in a writing mailed, or otherwise delivered, to the consumer, not later than three days after the date on which the report was first requested, and

(B) includes a statement informing the consumer of his right to request the additional disclosures provided for under subsection (b) of this section and the written summary of the rights of the consumer prepared pursuant to section 609(c) [§ 1681g]; and

(2) the person certifies or has certified to the consumer reporting agency that

(A) the person has made the disclosures to the consumer required by paragraph (1); and

(B) the person will comply with subsection (b).

(b) Disclosure on request of nature and scope of investigation. Any person who procures or causes to be prepared an investigative consumer report on any consumer shall, upon written request made by the consumer within a reasonable period of time after the receipt by him of the disclosure required by subsection (a)(1) of this section, make a complete and accurate disclosure of the nature and scope of the investigation requested. This disclosure shall be made in a writing mailed, or otherwise delivered, to the consumer not later than five days after the date on which the request for such disclosure was received from the consumer or such report was first requested, whichever is the later.

(c) Limitation on liability upon showing of reasonable procedures for compliance with provisions. No person may be held liable for any violation of subsection (a) or (b) of this section if he shows by a preponderance of the evidence that at the time of the violation he maintained reasonable procedures to assure compliance with subsection (a) or (b) of this section.

(d) Prohibitions.

    (1) Certification. A consumer reporting agency shall not prepare or furnish investigative consumer report unless the agency has received a certification under subsection (a)(2) from the person who requested the report.

    (2) Inquiries. A consumer reporting agency shall not make an inquiry for the purpose of preparing an investigative consumer report on a consumer for employment purposes if the making of the inquiry by an employer or prospective employer of the consumer would violate any applicable Federal or State equal employment opportunity law or regulation.

    (3) Certain public record information. Except as otherwise provided in section 613 [§ 1681k], a consumer reporting agency shall not furnish an investigative consumer report that includes information that is a matter of public record and that relates to an arrest, indictment, conviction, civil judicial action, tax lien, or outstanding judgment, unless the agency has verified the accuracy of the information during the 30-day period ending on the date on which the report is furnished.

    (4) Certain adverse information. A consumer reporting agency shall not prepare or furnish an investigative consumer report on a consumer that contains information that is adverse to the interest of the consumer and that is obtained through a personal interview with a neighbor, friend, or associate of the consumer or with

another person with whom the consumer is acquainted or who has knowledge of such item of information,
unless

(A) the agency has followed reasonable procedures to
obtain confirmation of the information, from an
additional source that has independent and direct
knowledge of the information; or

(B) the person interviewed is the best possible source
of the information.

§ 607. Compliance procedures [15 U.S.C. § 1681e]

(a) Identity and purposes of credit users. Every consumer-
reporting agency shall maintain reasonable procedures
designed to avoid violations of section 605 [§ 1681c] and
to limit the furnishing of consumer reports to the purposes
listed under section 604 [§ 1681b] of this title. These procedures shall require that prospective users of the information identify themselves, certify the purposes for which the
information is sought, and certify that the information will
be used for no other purpose. Every consumer reporting
agency shall make a reasonable effort to verify the identity
of a new prospective user and the uses certified by such
prospective user prior to furnishing such user a consumer
report. No consumer reporting agency may furnish a consumer report to any person if it has reasonable grounds for
believing that the consumer report will not be used for a
purpose listed in section 604 [§ 1681b] of this title.

(b) Accuracy of report. Whenever a consumer reporting agency prepares a consumer report it shall follow reasonable
procedures to assure maximum possible accuracy of the

information concerning the individual about whom the report relates.

(c) Disclosure of consumer reports by users allowed. A consumer reporting agency may not prohibit a user of a consumer report furnished by the agency on a consumer from disclosing the contents of the report to the consumer, if adverse action against the consumer has been taken by the user based in whole or in part on the report.

(d) Notice to users and furnishers of information.

  (1) Notice requirement. A consumer reporting agency shall provide to any person

    (A) who regularly and in the ordinary course of business furnishes information to the agency with respect to any consumer; or

    (B) to whom a consumer report is provided by the agency; a notice of such person's responsibilities under this title.

  (2) Content of notice. The Federal Trade Commission shall prescribe the content of notices under paragraph (1), and a consumer reporting agency shall be in compliance with this subsection if it provides a notice under paragraph (1) that is substantially similar to the Federal Trade Commission prescription under this paragraph.

(e) Procurement of consumer report for resale.

  (1) Disclosure. A person may not procure a consumer report for purposes of reselling the report (or any information in the report) unless the person discloses to the consumer reporting agency that originally fur-

nishes the report

   (A) the identity of the end-user of the report (or information); and

   (B) each permissible purpose under section 604 [§ 1681b] for which the report is furnished to the end-user of the report (or information).

(2) Responsibilities of procurers for resale. A person who procures a consumer report for purposes of reselling the report (or any information in the report) shall

   (A) establish and comply with reasonable procedures designed to ensure that the report (or information) is resold by the person only for a purpose for which the report may be furnished under section 604 [§ 1681b], including by requiring that each person to which the report (or information) is resold and that resells or provides the report (or information) to any other person

     (i) identifies each end user of the resold report (or information);

     (ii) certifies each purpose for which the report (or information) will be used; and

     (iii) certifies that the report (or information) will be used for no other purpose; and

   (B) before reselling the report, make reasonable efforts to verify the identifications and certifications made under subparagraph (A).

(3) Resale of consumer report to a federal agency or department. Notwithstanding paragraph (1) or (2), a person who procures a consumer report for purposes of reselling the report (or any information in the report) shall not disclose the identity of the end-user

of the report under paragraph (1) or (2) if–

(A) the end user is an agency or department of the United States Government which procures the reportfrom the person for purposes of determining the eligibility of the consumer concerned to receive access or continued access to classified information (as defined in section 604(b)(4)(E)(i)); and

(B) the agency or department certifies in writing to the person reselling the report that nondisclosure is necessary to protect classified information or the safety of persons employed by or contracting with, or undergoing investigation for work or contracting with the agency or department.

§ 608. Disclosures to governmental agencies [15 U.S.C. § 1681f]

Notwithstanding the provisions of section 604 [§ 1681b] of this title, a consumer reporting agency may furnish identifying information respecting any consumer, limited to his name, address, former addresses, places of employment, or former places of employment, to a governmental agency.

§ 609. Disclosures to consumers [15 U.S.C. § 1681g]

(a) Information on file; sources; report recipients. Every consumer reporting agency shall, upon request, and subject to 610(a)(1) [§ 1681h], clearly and accurately disclose to the consumer:

(1) All information in the consumer's file at the time of the request, except that nothing in this paragraph shall

be construed to require a consumer reporting agency to disclose to a consumer any information concerning credit scores or any other risk scores or predictors relating to the consumer.

(2) The sources of the information; except that the sources of information acquired solely for use in preparing an investigative consumer report and actually used for no other purpose need not be disclosed: Provided, that in the event an action is brought under this title, such sources shall be available to the plaintiff under appropriate discovery procedures in the court in which the action is brought.

(3) (A) Identification of each person (including each end-user identified under section 607(e)(1) [§ 1681e]) that procured a consumer report

    (i) for employment purposes, during the 2-year period preceding the date on which the request is made; or

    (ii) for any other purpose, during the 1-year period preceding the date on which the request is made.

(B) An identification of a person under subparagraph (A) shall include

    (i) the name of the person or, if applicable, the trade name (written in full) under which such person conducts business; and

    (ii) upon request of the consumer, the address and telephone number of the person.

(C) Subparagraph (A) does not apply if–

    (i) the end user is an agency or department of

the United States Government that procure the report from the person for purposes of determining the eligibility of the consumer to whom the report relates to receive access or continued access to classified information (as defined in section 604(b)(4)(E)(i)); and

(ii) the head of the agency or department makes a written finding as prescribed under section 604(b)(4)(A).

(4) The dates, original payees, and amounts of any checks upon which is based any adverse characterization of the consumer, included in the file at the time of the disclosure.

(5) A record of all inquiries received by the agency during the 1-year period preceding the request that identified the consumer in connection with a credit or insurance transaction that was not initiated by the consumer.

(b) Exempt information. The requirements of subsection (a) of this section respecting the disclosure of sources of information and the recipients of consumer reports do not apply to information received or consumer reports furnished prior to the effective date of this title except to the extent that the matter involved is contained in the files of the consumer reporting agency on that date.

(c) Summary of rights required to be included with disclosure.

(1) Summary of rights. A consumer reporting agency shall provide to a consumer, with each written disclosure by the agency to the consumer under this section

(A) a written summary of all of the rights that the

consumer has under this title; and

(B) in the case of a consumer reporting agency that compiles and maintains files on consumers on a nationwide basis, a toll-free telephone number established by the agency, at which personnel are accessible to consumers during normal business hours.

(2) Specific items required to be included. The summary of rights required under paragraph (1) shall include

(A) a brief description of this title and all rights of consumers under this title;

(B) an explanation of how the consumer may exercise the rights of the consumer under this title;

(C) a list of all Federal agencies responsible for enforcing any provision of this title and the address and any appropriate phone number of each such agency, in a form that will assist the consumer in selecting the appropriate agency;

(D) a statement that the consumer may have additional rights under State law and that the consumer may wish to contact a State or local consumer protection agency or a State attorney general to learn of those rights; and

(E) a statement that a consumer reporting agency is not required to remove accurate derogatory information from a consumer's file, unless the information is outdated under section 605 [§ 1681c] or cannot be verified.

(3) Form of summary of rights. For purposes of this subsection and any disclosure by a consumer reporting agency required under this title with

respect to consumers' rights, the Federal Trade Commission (after consultation with each Federal agency referred to in section 621(b) [§ 1681s]) shall prescribe the form and content of any such disclosure of the rights of consumers required under this title. A consumer reporting agency shall be in compliance with this subsection if it provides disclosures under paragraph (1) that are substantially similar to the Federal Trade Commission prescription under this paragraph.

(4) Effectiveness. No disclosures shall be required under this subsection until the date on which the Federal Trade Commission prescribes the form and content of such disclosures under paragraph (3).

§ 610. Conditions and form of disclosure to consumers [15 U.S.C. § 1681h]

(a) In general.

(1) Proper identification. A consumer reporting agency shall require, as a condition of making the disclosures required under section 609 [§ 1681g], that the consumer furnish proper identification.

(2) Disclosure in writing. Except as provided in subsection (b), the disclosures required to be made under section 609 [§ 1681g] shall be provided under that section in writing.

(b) Other forms of disclosure.

(1) In general. If authorized by a consumer, a consumer reporting agency may make the disclosures required under 609 [§ 1681g]

(A) other than in writing; and

      (B) in such form as may be

          (i) specified by the consumer in accordance with paragraph (2); and

          (ii) available from the agency.

  (2) Form. A consumer may specify pursuant to paragraph (1) that disclosures under section 609 [§ 1681g] shall be made

      (A) in person, upon the appearance of the consumer at the place of business of the consumer reporting agency where disclosures are regularly provided, during normal business hours, and on reasonable notice;

      (B) by telephone, if the consumer has made a written request for disclosure by telephone;

      (C) by electronic means, if available from the agency; or

      (D) by any other reasonable means that is available from the agency.

(c) Trained personnel. Any consumer reporting agency shall provide trained personnel to explain to the consumer any information furnished to him pursuant to section 609 [§ 1681g] of this title.

(d) Persons accompanying consumer. The consumer shall be permitted to be accompanied by one other person of his choosing, who shall furnish reasonable identification. A consumer reporting agency may require the consumer to furnish a written statement granting permission to the consumer reporting agency to discuss the consumer's file in such person's presence.

(e) Limitation of liability. Except as provided in sections 616 and 617 [§§ 1681n and 1681o] of this title, no consumer may bring any action or proceeding in the nature of defamation, invasion of privacy, or negligence with respect to the reporting of information against any consumer reporting agency, any user of information, or any person who furnishes information to a consumer reporting agency, based on information disclosed pursuant to section 609, 610, or 615 [§§ 1681g, 1681h, or 1681m] of this title or based on information disclosed by a user of a consumer report to or for a consumer against whom the user has taken adverse action, based in whole or in part on the report, except as to false information furnished with malice or willful intent to injure such consumer.

§ 611. Procedure in case of disputed accuracy [15 U.S.C. § 1681i]

(a) Reinvestigations of disputed information.

(1) Reinvestigation required.

(A) In general. If the completeness or accuracy of any item of information contained in a consumer's file at a consumer reporting agency is disputed by the consumer and the consumer notifies the agency directly of such dispute, the agency shall reinvestigate free of charge and record the current status of the disputed information, or delete the item from the file in accordance with paragraph (5), before the end of the 30-day period beginning on the date on which the agency receives the notice of the dispute from the consumer.

(B) Extension of period to reinvestigate. Except as provided in subparagraph (C), the 30-day period described in subparagraph (A) may be extended for not more than 15 additional days if the consumer reporting agency receives information from the consumer during that 30-day period that is relevant to the reinvestigation.

(C) Limitations on extension of period to reinvestigate. Subparagraph (B) shall not apply to any reinvestigation in which, during the 30-day period described in subparagraph (A), the information that is the subject of the reinvestigation is found to be inaccurate or incomplete or the consumer reporting agency determines that the information cannot be verified.

(2) Prompt notice of dispute to furnisher of information.

(A) In general. Before the expiration of the 5-business day period beginning on the date on which a consumer reporting agency receives notice of a dispute from any consumer in accordance with paragraph (1), the agency shall provide notification of the dispute to any person who provided any item of information in dispute, at the address and in the manner established with the person. The notice shall include all relevant information regarding the dispute that the agency has received from the consumer.

(B) Provision of other information from consumer. The consumer reporting agency shall promptly provide to the person who provided the information in dispute all relevant information regarding the dispute that is received by the agency from the consumer after the period referred to in subparagraph (A) and before the end of the period referred to in paragraph (1)(A).

(3) Determination that dispute is frivolous or irrelevant.

    (A) In general. Notwithstanding paragraph (1), a consumer reporting agency may terminate a reinvestigation of information disputed by a consumer under that paragraph if the agency reasonably determines that the dispute by the consumer is frivolous or irrelevant, including by reason of a failure by a consumer to provide sufficient information to investigate the disputed information.

    (B) Notice of determination. Upon making any determination in accordance with subparagraph (A) that a dispute is frivolous or irrelevant, a consumer reporting agency shall notify the consumer of such determination not later than 5 business days after making such determination, by mail or, if authorized by the consumer for that purpose, by any other means available to the agency.

    (C) Contents of notice. A notice under subparagraph (B) shall include

        (i) the reasons for the determination under subparagraph (A); and

        (ii) identification of any information required to investigate the disputed information, which may consist of a standardized form describing the general nature of such information.

(4) Consideration of consumer information. In conducting any reinvestigation under paragraph (1) with respect to disputed information in the file of any consumer, the consumer reporting agency shall review

and consider all relevant information submitted by the consumer in the period described in paragraph (1)(A) with respect to such disputed information.

(5) Treatment of inaccurate or unverifiable information.

    (A) In general. If, after any reinvestigation under paragraph (1) of any information disputed by a consumer, an item of the information is found to be inaccurate or incomplete or cannot be verified, the consumer reporting agency shall promptly delete that item of information from the consumer's file or modify that item of information, as appropriate, based on the results of the reinvestigation.

    (B) Requirements relating to reinsertion of previously deleted material.

        (i) Certification of accuracy of information. If any information is deleted from a consumer's file pursuant to subparagraph (A), the information may not be reinserted in the file by the consumer reporting agency unless the person who furnishes the information certifies that the information is complete and accurate.

        (ii) Notice to consumer. If any information that has been deleted from a consumer's file pursuant to subparagraph (A) is reinserted in the file, the consumer reporting agency shall notify the consumer of the reinsertion in writing not later than 5 business days after the reinsertion or, if authorized by the consumer for that purpose, by any other means available to the agency.

(iii) Additional information. As part of, or in addition to, the notice under clause (ii), a consumer reporting agency shall provide to a consumer in writing not later than 5 business days after the date of the reinsertion

    (I)   a statement that the disputed information has been reinserted;

    (II) the business name and address of any furnisher of information contacted and the telephone number of such furnisher, if reasonably available, or of any furnisher of information that contacted the consumer reporting agency, in connection with the reinsertion of such information; and

    (III) a notice that the consumer has the right to add a statement to the consumer's file disputing the accuracy or completeness of the disputed information.

C) Procedures to prevent reappearance. A consumer reporting agency shall maintain reasonable procedures designed to prevent the reappearance in a consumer's file, and in consumer reports on the consumer, of information that is deleted pursuant to this paragraph (other than information that is reinserted in accordance with subparagraph (B)(i)).

D) Automated reinvestigation system. Any consumer reporting agency that compiles and maintains files on consumers on a nationwide basis shall implement an automated system through which furnishers of information to that consumer reporting agency may report the results of a reinvestigation that finds incomplete or inaccurate information in a consumer's file to other such consumer reporting agencies.

(6) Notice of results of reinvestigation.

   (A) In general. A consumer reporting agency shall provide written notice to a consumer of the results of a reinvestigation under this subsection not later than 5 business days after the completion of the reinvestigation, by mail or, if authorized by the consumer for that purpose, by other means available to the agency.

   (B) Contents. As part of, or in addition to, the notice under subparagraph (A), a consumer reporting agency shall provide to a consumer in writing before the expiration of the 5-day period referred to in subparagraph (A)

      (i) a statement that the reinvestigation is completed;

      (ii) a consumer report that is based upon the consumer's file as that file is revised as a result of the reinvestigation;

      (iii) a notice that, if requested by the consumer, a description of the procedure used to determine the accuracy and completeness of the information shall be provided to the consumer by the agency, including the business name and address of any furnisher of information contacted in connection with such information and the telephone number of such furnisher, if reasonably available;

(iv) a notice that the consumer has the right to add a statement to the consumer's file disputing the accuracy or completeness of the information; and

(v) a notice that the consumer has the right to request under subsection (d) that the consumer reporting agency furnish notifications under that subsection.

(7) Description of reinvestigation procedure. A consumer reporting agency shall provide to a consumer a description referred to in paragraph (6)(B)(iii) by not later than 15 days after receiving a request from the consumer for that description.

(8) Expedited dispute resolution. If a dispute regarding an item of information in a consumer's file at a consumer reporting agency is resolved in accordance with paragraph (5)(A) by the deletion of the disputed information by not later than 3 business days after the date on which the agency receives notice of the dispute from the consumer in accordance with paragraph (1)(A), then the agency shall not be required to comply with paragraphs (2), (6), and (7) with respect to that dispute if the agency

(A) provides prompt notice of the deletion to the consumer by telephone;

(B) includes in that notice, or in a written notice that accompanies a confirmation and consumer report provided in accordance with subparagraph (C), a statement of the consumer's right to request under subsection (d) that the agency furnish notifications under that subsection; and

(C) provides written confirmation of the deletion and a copy of a consumer report on the consumer that is based on the consumer's file after the deletion, not later than 5 business days after making the deletion.

(b) Statement of dispute. If the reinvestigation does not resolve the dispute, the consumer may file a brief statement setting forth the nature of the dispute. The consumer reporting agency may limit such statements to not more than one hundred words if it provides the consumer with assistance in writing a clear summary of the dispute.

(c) Notification of consumer dispute in subsequent consumer-reports. Whenever a statement of a dispute is filed, unless there is reasonable grounds to believe that it is frivolous or irrelevant, the consumer reporting agency shall, in any subsequent consumer report containing the information in question, clearly note that it is disputed by the consumer and provide either the consumer's statement or a clear and accurate codification or summary thereof.

(d) Notification of deletion of disputed information. Following any deletion of information which is found to be inaccurate or whose accuracy can no longer be verified or any notation as to disputed information, the consumer reporting agency shall, at the request of the consumer, furnish notification that the item has been deleted or the statement, codification or summary pursuant to subsection (b) or (c) of this section to any person specifically designated by the consumer who has within two years prior thereto received a consumer report for employment purposes, or within six months prior thereto received a consumer report for any other purpose, which contained the deleted or disputed information.

§ 612. Charges for certain disclosures [15 U.S.C. § 1681j]

(a) Reasonable charges allowed for certain disclosures.

    (1) In general. Except as provided in subsections (b), (c), and (d), a consumer reporting agency may impose a reasonable charge on a consumer

        (A) for making a disclosure to the consumer pursuant to section 609 [§ 1681g], which charge

            (i) shall not exceed $8;(3) and

            (ii) shall be indicated to the consumer before making the disclosure; and

        (B) for furnishing, pursuant to 611(d) [§ 1681i], following a reinvestigation under section 611(a) [§ 1681i], a statement, codification, or summary to a person designated by the consumer under that section after the 30-day period beginning on the date of notification of the consumer under paragraph (6) or (8) of section 611(a) [§ 1681i] with respect to the reinvestigation, which charge

            (i) shall not exceed the charge that the agency would impose on each designated recipient for a consumer report; and

            (ii) shall be indicated to the consumer before furnishing such information.

    (2) Modification of amount. The Federal Trade

Commission shall increase the amount referred to in paragraph (1)(A)(I) on January 1 of each year, based proportionally on changes in the Consumer Price Index, with fractional changes rounded to the nearest fifty cents.

(b) Free disclosure after adverse notice to consumer. Each consumer consumer reporting agency that maintains a file on a consumer shall make all disclosures pursuant to section 609 [§ 1681g] without charge to the consumer if, not later than 60 days after receipt by such consumer of a notification pursuant to section 615 [§ 1681m], or of a notification from a debt collection agency affiliated with that consumer reporting agency stating that the consumer's credit rating may be or has been adversely affected, the consumer makes a request under section 609 [§ 1681g].

(c) Free disclosure under certain other circumstances. Upon the request of the consumer, a consumer reporting agency shall make all disclosures pursuant to section 609 [§ 1681g] once during any 12-month period without charge to that consumer if the consumer certifies in writing that the consumer

  (1) is unemployed and intends to apply for employment in the 60-day period beginning on the date on which the certification is made;

  (2) is a recipient of public welfare assistance; or

  (3) has reason to believe that the file on the consumer at the agency contains inaccurate information due to fraud.

(d) Other charges prohibited. A consumer reporting agency

shall not impose any charge on a consumer for providing any notification required by this title or making any disclosure required by this title, except as authorized by subsection (a).

§ 613. Public record information for employment purposes [15 U.S.C. § 1681k]

(a) In general. A consumer reporting agency which furnishes a consumer report for employment purposes and which for that purpose compiles and reports items of information on consumers which are matters of public record and are likely to have an adverse effect upon a consumer's ability to obtain employment shall

   (1) at the time such public record information is reported to the user of such consumer report, notify the consumer of the fact that public record information is being reported by the consumer reporting agency, together with the name and address of the person to whom such information is being reported; or

   (2) maintain strict procedures designed to insure that whenever public record information which is likely to have an adverse effect on a consumer's ability to obtain employment is reported it is complete and up to date. For purposes of this paragraph, items of public record relating to arrests, indictments, convictions, suits, tax liens, and outstanding judgments shall be considered up to date if the current public record status of the item at the time of the report is reported.

(b) Exemption for national security investigations. Subsection (a) does not apply in the case of an agency or department of the United States Government that seeks to obtain and use a consumer report for employment purposes, if the head of the agency or department makes a written finding as prescribed under section 604(b)(4)(A).

§ 614. Restrictions on investigative consumer reports [15 U.S.C. § 1681l]

Whenever a consumer reporting agency prepares an investigative consumer report, no adverse information in the consumer report (other than information which is a matter of public record) may be included in a subsequent consumer report unless such adverse information has been verified in the process of making such subsequent consumer report, or the adverse information was received within the three-month period preceding the date the subsequent report is furnished.

§ 615. Requirements on users of consumer reports [15 U.S.C. § 1681m]

(a) Duties of users taking adverse actions on the basis of information contained in consumer reports. If any person takes any adverse action with respect to any consumer that is based in whole or in part on any information contained in a consumer report, the person shall

   (1) provide oral, written, or electronic notice of the adverse action to the consumer;

   (2) provide to the consumer orally, in writing, or electronically

      (A) the name, address, and telephone number of the consumer reporting agency (including a toll-free telephone number established by the agency if the agency compiles and maintains files on consumers on a nationwide basis) that furnished the report to the person; and

(B) a statement that the consumer reporting agency did not make the decision to take the adverse action and is unable to provide the consumer the specific reasons why the adverse action was taken; and

(3) provide to the consumer an oral, written, or electronic notice of the consumer's right

(A) to obtain, under section 612 [§ 1681j], a free copy of a consumer report on the consumer from the consumer reporting agency referred to in paragraph (2), which notice shall include an indication of the 60-day period under that section for obtaining such a copy; and

(B) to dispute, under section 611 [§ 1681i], with a consumer reporting agency the accuracy or completeness of any information in a consumer report furnished by the agency.

(b) Adverse action based on information obtained from thir parties other than consumer reporting agencies.

(1) In general. Whenever credit for personal, family, or household purposes involving a consumer is denied or the charge for such credit is increased either wholly or partly because of information obtained from a person other than a consumer reporting agency bearing upon the consumer's credit worthiness, credit standing, credit capacity, character, general reputation, personal characteristics, or mode of living, the user of such information shall, within a reasonable period of time,

upon the consumer's written request for the reasons for such adverse action received within sixty days after learning of such adverse action, disclose the nature of the information to the consumer. The user of such information shall clearly and accurately disclose to the consumer his right to make such written request at the time such adverse action is communicated to the consumer.

(2) Duties of person taking certain actions based on information provided by affiliate.

    (A) Duties, generally. If a person takes an action described in subparagraph (B) with respect to a consumer, based in whole or in part on information described in subparagraph (C), the person shall

        (i) notify the consumer of the action, including a statement that the consumer may obtain the information in accordance with clause (ii); and

        (ii) upon a written request from the consumer received within 60 days after transmittal of the notice required by clause (I), disclose to the consumer the nature of the information upon which the action is based by not later than 30 days after receipt of the request.

    (B) Action described. An action referred to in subparagraph (A) is an adverse action described in section 603(k)(1)(A) [§ 1681a], taken in connection with a transaction initiated by the consumer, or any adverse action described in clause (i) or (ii) of section 603(k)(1)(B) [§ 1681a].

    (C) Information described. Information referred to in

subparagraph (A)

(i) except as provided in clause (ii), is information that

    (I) is furnished to the person taking the action by a person related by common ownership or affiliated by common corporate control to the person taking the action; and

    (II) bears on the credit worthiness, credit standing, credit capacity, character, general reputation, personal characteristics, or mode of living of the consumer; and

(ii) does not include

    (I) information solely as to transactions or experiences between the consumer and the person furnishing the information; or

    (II) information in a consumer report.

(c) Reasonable procedures to assure compliance. No person shall be held liable for any violation of this section if he shows by a preponderance of the evidence that at the time of the alleged violation he maintained reasonable procedures to assure compliance with the provisions of this section.

(d) Duties of users making written credit or insurance solicitations on the basis of information contained in consumer files.

(1) In general. Any person who uses a consumer report on any consumer in connection with any credit or insurance transaction that is not initiated by the consumer, that is provided to that person under section

604(c)(1)(B) [§ 1681b], shall provide with each written solicitation made to the consumer regarding the transaction a clear and conspicuous statement that

(A) information contained in the consumer's consumer report was used in connection with the transaction;

(B) the consumer received the offer of credit or insurance because the consumer satisfied the criteria for credit worthiness or insurability under which the consumer was selected for the offer;

(C) if applicable, the credit or insurance may not be extended if, after the consumer responds to the offer, the consumer does not meet the criteria used to select the consumer for the offer or any applicable criteria bearing on credit worthiness or insurability or does not furnish any required collateral;

(D) the consumer has a right to prohibit information contained in the consumer's file with any consumer reporting agency from being used in connection with any credit or insurance transaction that is not initiated by the consumer; and (E) the consumer may exercise the right referred to in subparagraph (D) by notifying a notification system established under section 604(e) [§ 1681b].

(2) Disclosure of address and telephone number. A statement under paragraph (1) shall include the address and toll-free telephone number of the appropriate notification system established under section 604(e) [§ 1681b].

(3) Maintaining criteria on file. A person who makes an

offer of credit or insurance to a consumer under a credit or insurance transaction described in paragraph (1) shall maintain on file the criteria used to select the consumer to receive the offer, all criteria bearing on credit worthiness or insurability, as applicable, that are the basis for determining whether or not to extend credit or insurance pursuant to the offer, and any requirement for the furnishing of collateral as a condition of the extension of credit or insurance, until the expiration of the 3-year period beginning on the date on which the offer is made to the consumer.

(4) Authority of federal agencies regarding unfair or deceptive acts or practices not affected. This section is not intended to affect the authority of any Federal or State agency to enforce a prohibition against unfair or deceptive acts or practices, including the making of false or misleading statements in connection with a credit or insurance transaction that is not initiated by the consumer.

§ 616. Civil liability for willful noncompliance [15 U.S.C. § 1681n]

(a) In general. Any person who willfully fails to comply with any requirement imposed under this title with respect to any consumer is liable to that consumer in an amount equal to the sum of (1)(A) any actual damages sustained by the consumer as a result of the failure or damages of not less than $100 and not more than $1,000; or (B) in the case of liability of a natural person for obtaining a consumer report under false pretenses or knowingly without a permissible purpose, actual damages sustained by the consumer as a result of the failure or $1,000, whichever is greater; (2) such amount of punitive damages as the court may allow; and (3) in the case of any successful action to enforce any liability under this section, the costs of the action together with reasonable attorney's fees as determined by the court.

(b) Civil liability for knowing noncompliance. Any person who obtains a consumer report from a consumer reporting agency under false pretenses or knowingly without a permissible purpose shall be liable to the consumer reporting agency for actual damages sustained by the consumer reporting agency or $1,000, whichever is greater.

(c) Attorney's fees. Upon a finding by the court that an unsuccessful pleading, motion, or other paper filed in connection with an action under this section was filed in bad faith or for purposes of harassment, the court shall award to the prevailing party attorney's fees reasonable in relation to the work expended in responding to the pleading, motion, or other paper.

§ 617. Civil liability for negligent noncompliance [15 U.S.C. § 1681o]

(a) In general. Any person who is negligent in failing to comply with any requirement imposed under this title with respect to any consumer is liable to that consumer in an amount equal to the sum of

(1) any actual damages sustained by the consumer as a result of the failure;

(2) in the case of any successful action to enforce any liability under this section, the costs of the action together with reasonable attorney's fees as determined

by the court.

(b) Attorney's fees. On a finding by the court that an unsuccessful pleading, motion, or other paper filed in connection with an action under this section was filed in bad faith or for purposes of harassment, the court shall award to the prevailing party attorney's fees reasonable in relation to the work expended in responding to the pleading, motion, or other paper.

§ 618. Jurisdiction of courts; limitation of actions [15 U.S.C. § 1681p]

An action to enforce any liability created under this title may be brought in any appropriate United States district court without regard to the amount in controversy, or in any other court of competent jurisdiction, within two years from the date on which the liability arises, except that where a defendant has materially and willfully misrepresented any information required under this title to be disclosed to an individual and the information so misrepresented is material to the establishment of the defendant's liability to that individual under this title, the action may be brought at any time within two years after discovery by the individual of the misrepresentation.

§ 619. Obtaining information under false pretenses [15 U.S.C. § 1681q]

Any person who knowingly and willfully obtains information on a consumer from a consumer reporting agency under false pretenses shall be fined under title 18, United States Code, imprisoned for not more than 2 years, or both.

§ 620. Unauthorized disclosures by officers or employ-

ees [15 U.S.C. § 1681r]

Any officer or employee of a consumer reporting agency who knowingly and willfully provides information concerning an individual from the agency's files to a person not authorized to receive that information shall be fined under title 18, United States Code, imprisoned for not more than 2 years, or both.

§ 621. Administrative enforcement [15 U.S.C. § 1681s]

(a) (1) Enforcement by Federal Trade Commission. Compliance with the requirements imposed under this title shall be enforced under the Federal Trade Commission Act [15 U.S.C. §§ 41 et seq.] by the Federal Trade Commission with respect to consumer reporting agencies and all other persons subject thereto, except to the extent that enforcement of the requirements imposed under this title is specifically committed to some other government agency under subsection (b) hereof. For the purpose of the exercise by the Federal Trade Commission of its functions and powers under the Federal Trade Commission Act, a violation of any requirement or prohibition imposed under this title shall constitute an unfair or deceptive act or practice in commerce in violation of section 5(a) of the Federal Trade Commission Act [15 U.S.C. § 45(a)] and shall be subject to enforcement by the Federal Trade Commission under section 5(b) thereof [15 U.S.C. § 45(b)] with respect to any consumer reporting agency or person subject to enforcement by the Federal Trade Commission pursuant to this subsection, irrespective of whether that person is engaged in commerce or meets any other jurisdictional tests in the Federal Trade

Commission Act. The Federal Trade Commission shall have such procedural, investigative, and enforcement powers, including the power to issue procedural rules in enforcing compliance with the requirements imposed under this title and to require the filing of reports, the production of documents, and the appearance of witnesses as though the applicable terms and conditions of the Federal Trade Commission Act were part of this title. Any person violating any of the provisions of this title shall be subject to the penalties and entitled to the privileges and immunities provided in the Federal Trade Commission Act as though the applicable terms and provisions thereof were part of this title. (2)(A) In the event of a knowing violation, which constitutes a pattern or practice of violations of this title, the Commission may commence a civil action to recover a civil penalty in a district court of the United States against any person that violates this title. In such action, such person shall be liable for a civil penalty of not more than $2,500 per violation. (B) In determining the amount of a civil penalty under subparagraph (A), the court shall take into account the degree of culpability, any history of prior such conduct, ability to pay, effect on ability to continue to do business, and such other matters as justice may require. (3) Notwithstanding paragraph (2), a court may not impose any civil penalty on a person for a violation of section 623(a)(1) [§ 1681s-2] unless the person has been enjoined from committing the violation, or ordered not to commit the violation, in an action or proceeding brought by or on behalf of the Federal Trade Commission, and has violated the injunction or order, and the court may not impose any civil penalty for any violation occurring before the date of the violation of the injunction or order.

(b) Enforcement by other agencies. Compliance with the requirements imposed under this title with respect to consumer reporting agencies, persons who use consumer reports from such agencies, persons who furnish information to such agencies, and users of information that are subject to subsection (d) of section 615 [§ 1681m] shall be enforced under

    (1) section 8 of the Federal Deposit Insurance Act [12 U.S.C. § 1818], in the case of

        (A) national banks, and Federal branches and Federal agencies of foreign banks, by the Office of the Comptroller of the Currency;

        (B) member banks of the Federal Reserve System (other than national banks), branches and agencies of foreign banks (other than Federal branches, Federal agencies, and insured State branches of foreign banks), commercial lending companies owned or controlled by foreign banks, and organizations operating under section 25 or 25(a) [25A] of the Federal Reserve Act [12 U.S.C. §§ 601 et seq., §§ 611 et seq], by the Board of Governors of the Federal Reserve System; and

        (C) banks insured by the Federal Deposit Insurance Corporation (other than members of the Federal Reserve System) and insured State branches of foreign banks, by the Board of Directors of the Federal Deposit Insurance Corporation;

    (2) section 8 of the Federal Deposit Insurance Act [12 U.S.C. § 1818], by the Director of the Office of Thrift

Supervision, in the case of a savings association the deposits of which are insured by the Federal Deposit Insurance Corporation;

(3) the Federal Credit Union Act [12 U.S.C. §§ 1751 et seq.], by the Administrator of the National Credit Union Administration [National Credit Union Administration Board] with respect to any Federal credit union;

(4) subtitle IV of title 49 [49 U.S.C. §§ 10101 et seq.], by the Secretary of Transportation, with respect to all carriers subject to the jurisdiction of the Surface Transportation Board;

(5) the Federal Aviation Act of 1958 [49 U.S.C. Appx §§ 1301 et seq.], by the Secretary of Transportation with respect to any air carrier or foreign air carrier subject to that Act [49 U.S.C. Appx §§ 1301 et seq.]; and

(6) the Packers and Stockyards Act, 1921 [7 U.S.C. §§ 181 et seq.] (except as provided in section 406 of that Act [7 U.S.C. §§ 226 and 227]), by the Secretary of Agriculture with respect to any activities subject to that Act.

The terms used in paragraph (1) that are not defined in this title or otherwise defined in section 3(s) of the Federal Deposit Insurance Act (12 U.S.C. §1813(s)) shall have the meaning given to them in section 1(b) of the International Banking Act of 1978 (12 U.S.C. § 3101).

(c) State action for violations.

(1) Authority of states. In addition to such other remedies as are provided under State law, if the chief law enforcement officer of a State, or an official or agency designated by a State, has reason to believe that any

person has violated or is violating this title, the State

(A) may bring an action to enjoin such violation in any appropriate United States district court or in any other court of competent jurisdiction;

(B) subject to paragraph (5), may bring an action on behalf of the residents of the State to recover

(i) damages for which the person is liable to such residents under sections 616 and 617 [§§ 1681n and 1681o] as a result of the violation;

(ii) in the case of a violation of section 623(a) [§ 1681s-2], damages for which the person would, but for section 623(c) [§ 1681s-2], be liable to such residents as a result of the violation; or

(iii) damages of not more than $1,000 for each willful or negligent violation; and

(C) in the case of any successful action under subparagraph (A) or (B), shall be awarded the costs of the action and reasonable attorney fees as determined by the court.

(2) Rights of federal regulators. The State shall serve prior written notice of any action under paragraph (1) upon the Federal Trade Commission or the appropriate Federal regulator determined under subsection (b) and provide the Commission or appropriate Federal regulator with a copy of its complaint, except in any case in which such prior notice is not feasible, in which case the State shall serve such notice immediately upon instituting such action. The Federal Trade Commission or appropriate Federal regulator shall have the right

    (A) to intervene in the action;

    (B) upon so intervening, to be heard on all matters arising therein;

    (C) to remove the action to the appropriate United States district court; and

    (D) to file petitions for appeal.

(3) Investigatory powers. For purposes of bringing any action under this subsection, nothing in this subsection shall prevent the chief law enforcement officer, or an official or agency designated by a State, from exercising the powers conferred on the chief law enforcement officer or such official by the laws of such State to conduct investigations or to administer oaths or affirmations or to compel the attendance of witnesses or the production of documentary and other evidence.

(4) Limitation on state action while federal action pending. If the Federal Trade Commission or the appropriate Federal regulator has instituted a civil action or an administrative action under section 8 of the Federal Deposit Insurance Act for a violation of this title, no State may, during the pendency of such action, bring an action under this section against any defendant named in the complaint of the Commission or the appropriate Federal regulator for any violation of this title that is alleged in that complaint.

(5) Limitations on state actions for violation of section 623(a)(1) [§ 1681s-2].

    (A) Violation of injunction required. A State may not bring an action against a person under paragrap(1)(B) for a violation of section 623(a)(1)

[§ 1681s-2], unless

(i) the person has been enjoined from committing the violation, in an action brought by the State under paragraph (1)(A); and

(ii) the person has violated the injunction.

(B) Limitation on damages recoverable. In an action against a person under paragraph (1)(B) for a violation of section 623(a)(1) [§ 1681s-2], a State may not recover any damages incurred before the date of the violation of an injunction on which the action is based.

(d) Enforcement under other authority. For the purpose of the exercise by any agency referred to in subsection (b) of this section of its powers under any Act referred to in that subsection, a violation of any requirement imposed under this title shall be deemed to be a violation of a requirement imposed under that Act. In addition to its powers under any provision of law specifically referred to in subsection (b) of this section, each of the agencies referred to in that subsection may exercise, for the purpose of enforcing compliance with any requirement imposed under this title any other authority conferred on it by law.

(e) Regulatory authority

(1) The Federal banking agencies referred to in paragraphs (1) and (2) of subsection (b) shall jointly prescribe such regulations as necessary to carry out the purposes of this Act with respect to any persons identified under paragraphs (1) and (2) of subsection (b), and the Board of Governors of the Federal Reserve System shall have authority to prescribe regulations consistent

with such joint regulations with respect to bank holding companies and affiliates (other than depository
institutions and consumer reporting agencies) of such
holding companies.

(2) The Board of the National Credit Union
Administration shall prescribe such regulations as
necessary to carry out the purposes of this Act with
respect to any persons identified under paragraph (3)
of subsection (b).

§ 622. Information on overdue child support obligations [15 U.S.C. § 1681s-1]

Notwithstanding any other provision of this title, a consumer
reporting agency shall include in any consumer report furnished
by the agency in accordance with section 604 [§ 1681b] of this
title, any information on the failure of the consumer to pay overdue support which

(1) is provided

(A) to the consumer reporting agency by a State or
local child support enforcement agency; or

(B) to the consumer reporting agency and verified by
any local, State, or Federal government agency;
and

(2) antedates the report by 7 years or less.

§ 623. Responsibilities of furnishers of information to consumer reporting agencies [15 U.S.C. § 1681s-2]

(a) Duty of furnishers of information to provide accurate
information.

(1) Prohibition.

(A) Reporting information with actual knowledge of errors. A person shall not furnish any information relating to a consumer to any consumer reporting agency if the person knows or consciously avoids knowing that the information is inaccurate.

(B) Reporting information after notice and confirmation of errors. A person shall not furnish information relating to a consumer to any consumer reporting agency if

(i) the person has been notified by the consumer, at the address specified by the person for such notices, that specific information is inaccurate; and

(ii) the information is, in fact, inaccurate.

(C) No address requirement. A person who clearly and conspicuously specifies to the consumer an address for notices referred to in subparagraph (B) shall not be subject to subparagraph (A); however, nothing in subparagraph (B) shall require a person to specify such an address.

(2) Duty to correct and update information. A person who

(A) regularly and in the ordinary course of business furnishes information to one or more consumer reporting agencies about the person's transactions or experiences with any consumer; and

(B) has furnished to a consumer reporting agency information that the person determines is not complete or accurate, shall promptly notify the consumer reporting agency of that determination and provide to the agency any corrections to that information, or any additional information, that is necessary to make the information provided by the person to the agency complete and accurate, and shall not thereafter furnish to the agency any of the information that remains not complete or accurate.

(3) Duty to provide notice of dispute. If the completeness or accuracy of any information furnished by any person to any consumer reporting agency is disputed to such person by a consumer, the person may not furnish the information to any consumer reporting agency without notice that such information is disputed by the consumer.

(4) Duty to provide notice of closed accounts. A person who regularly and in the ordinary course of business furnishes information to a consumer reporting agency regarding a consumer who has a credit account with that person shall notify the agency of the voluntary closure of the account by the consumer, in information regularly furnished for the period in which the account is closed.

(5) Duty to provide notice of delinquency of accounts. A person who furnishes information to a consumer reporting agency regarding a delinquent account being placed for collection, charged to profit or loss, or subjected to any similar action shall, not later than 90 days after furnishing the information, notify the agency of the month and year of the commencement of the delinquency that immediately preceded the action.

(b) Duties of furnishers of information upon notice of dispute.

(1) In general. After receiving notice pursuant to section 611(a)(2) [§ 1681i] of a dispute with regard to the

completeness or accuracy of any information provided by a person to a consumer reporting agency, the person shall

(A) conduct an investigation with respect to the disputed information;

(B) review all relevant information provided by the consumer reporting agency pursuant to section 611(a)(2) [§ 1681i];

(C) report the results of the investigation to the consumer reporting agency; and

(D) if the investigation finds that the information is incomplete or inaccurate, report those results to all other consumer reporting agencies to which the person furnished the information and that compile and maintain files on consumers on a nationwide basis.

(2) Deadline. A person shall complete all investigations, reviews, and reports required under paragraph (1) regarding information provided by the person to a consumer reporting agency, before the expiration of the period under section 611(a)(1) [§ 1681i] within which the consumer reporting agency is required to complete actions required by that section regarding that information.

(c) Limitation on liability. Sections 616 and 617 [§§ 1681n and 1681o] do not apply to any failure to comply with subsection (a), except as provided in section 621(c)(1)(B) [§ 1681s].

(d) Limitation on enforcement. Subsection (a) shall be enforced exclusively under section 621 [§ 1681s] by the

Federal agencies and officials and the State officials identified in that section.

§ 624. Relation to State laws [15 U.S.C. § 1681t]

(a) In general. Except as provided in subsections (b) and (c), this title does not annul, alter, affect, or exempt any person subject to the provisions of this title from complying with the laws of any State with respect to the collection, distribution, or use of any information on consumers, except to the extent that those laws are inconsistent with any provision of this title, and then only to the extent of the inconsistency.

(b) General exceptions. No requirement or prohibition may be imposed under the laws of any State

  (1) with respect to any subject matter regulated under

    (A) subsection (c) or (e) of section 604 [§ 1681b], relating to the prescreening of consumer reports;

    (B) section 611 [§ 1681i], relating to the time by which a consumer reporting agency must take any action, including the provision of notification to a consumer or other person, in any procedure related to the disputed accuracy of information in a consumer's file, except that this subparagraph shall not apply to any State law in effect on the date of enactment of the Consumer Credit Reporting Reform Act of 1996;

    (C) subsections (a) and (b) of section 615 [§ 1681m], relating to the duties of a person who takes any adverse action with respect to a consumer;

    (D) section 615(d) [§ 1681m], relating to the duties of persons who use a consumer report of a consumer in connection with any credit or insurance transaction that is not initiated by the consumer and that consists of a firm offer of credit or insurance;

(E)   section 605 [§ 1681c], relating to information-contained in consumer reports, except that this ubparagraph shall not apply to any State law in effect on the date of enactment of the Consumer Credit Reporting Reform Act of 1996; or

(F)   section 623 [§ 1681s-2], relating to the responsibilities of persons who furnish information to consumer reporting agencies, except that this paragraph shall not apply

   (i)   with respect to section 54A(a) of chapter 93 of the Massachusetts Annotated Laws (as in effect on the date of enactment of the Consumer Credit Reporting Reform Act of 1996); or

   (ii) with respect to section 1785.25(a) of the California Civil Code (as in effect on the date of enactment of the Consumer Credit Reporting Reform Act of 1996);

(2)   with respect to the exchange of information among persons affiliated by common ownership or common corporate control, except that this paragraph shall not apply with respect to subsection (a) or (c)(1) of section 2480e of title 9, Vermont Statutes Annotated (as in effect on the date of enactment of the Consumer Credit Reporting Reform Act of 1996); or

(3)   with respect to the form and content of any disclosure required to be made under section 609(c) [§ 1681g].

(c) Definition of firm offer of credit or insurance
Notwithstanding any definition of the term "firm offer of credit or insurance" (or any equivalent term) under the laws of any State, the definition of that term contained in section 603(l) [§ 1681a] shall be construed to apply in the enforcement and interpretation of the laws of any State governing consumer reports.

(d) Limitations. Subsections (b) and (c)

    (1) do not affect any settlement, agreement, or consent judgment between any State Attorney General and any consumer reporting agency in effect on the date of enactment of the Consumer Credit Reporting Reform Act of 1996; and

    (2) do not apply to any provision of State law (including any provision of a State constitution) that

        (A) is enacted after January 1, 2004;

        (B) states explicitly that the provision is intended to supplement this title; and

        (C) gives greater protection to consumers than is provided under this title.

§ 625. Disclosures to FBI for counterintelligence purposes [15 U.S.C. § 1681u]

(a) Identity of financial institutions. Notwithstanding section 604 [§ 1681b] or any other provision of this title, a consumer reporting agency shall furnish to the Federal Bureau of Investigation the names and addresses of all financial institutions (as that term is defined in section 1101 of the Right to Financial Privacy Act of 1978 [12 U.S.C. § 3401]) at which a consumer maintains or has maintained an account, to the extent that information is in the files of the agency, when presented with a written request for that information, signed by the Director of the Federal Bureau of Investigation, or the Director's designee in a position not lower than Deputy Assistant Director at Bureau headquarters or a Special Agent in Charge of a Bureau field office designated by the Director, which certifies compliance with this section. The Director or the Director's designee may make such a certification only if the Director or the Director's designee has determined in writing, that such information is sought for the conduct of an authorized investigation to protect against international terrorism or clandestine intelligence activities, provided that such an investigation of a United States person is not conducted solely upon the basis of activities protected by the first amendment to the Constitution of the United States.

(b) Identifying information. Notwithstanding the provisions of section 604 [§ 1681b] or any other provision of this title, a consumer reporting agency shall furnish identifying information respecting a consumer, limited to name, address, former addresses, places of employment, or former places of employment, to the Federal Bureau of Investigation when presented with a written request, signed by the Director or the Director's designee, which certifies compliance with this subsection. The Director or the Director's designee in a position not lower than Deputy Assistant Director at Bureau headquarters or a Special Agent in Charge of a Bureau field office designated by the Director may make such a certification only if the Director or the Director's designee has determined in writing that such information is sought for the conduct of an authorized investigation to protect against international terrorism or clandestine intelligence activities, provided that such an investigation of a United States person is not conducted solely upon the basis of activities protected by the first amendment to the Constitution of the United States.

(c) Court order for disclosure of consumer reports. Notwithstanding section 604 [§ 1681b] or any other provision of this title, if requested in writing by the Director of the Federal Bureau of Investigation, or a designee of the Director in a position not lower than Deputy Assistant Director at Bureau headquarters or a Special Agent in Charge of a Bureau field office designated by the Director, a court may issue an order ex parte directing a consumer reporting agency to furnish a consumer report to the Federal Bureau of Investigation, upon a showing in camera that the consumer report is sought for the conduct of an authorized investigation to protect against international terrorism or clandestine intelligence activities, provided that such an investigation of a United States person is not conducted solely upon the basis of activities protected by the first amendment to the Constitution of the United States. The terms of an order issued under this subsection shall not disclose that the order is issued for purposes of a counterintelligence investigation.

(d) Confidentiality. No consumer reporting agency or officer, employee, or agent of a consumer reporting agency shall disclose to any person, other than those officers, employees, or agents of a consumer reporting agency necessary to fulfill the requirement to disclose information to the Federal Bureau of Investigation under this section, that the Federal Bureau of Investigation has sought or obtained the identity of financial institutions or a consumer report respecting any consumer under subsection (a), (b), or (c), and no consumer reporting agency or officer, employee, or agent of a consumer reporting agency shall include in any consumer report any information that would indicate that the Federal Bureau of Investigation has sought or obtained such information or a consumer report.

(e) Payment of fees. The Federal Bureau of Investigation shall, subject to the availability of appropriations, pay to the consumer reporting agency assembling or providing report or information in accordance with procedures established under this section a fee for reimbursement for such costs as are reasonably necessary and which have been directly incurred in searching, reproducing, or transporting books, papers, records, or other data required or requested to be produced under this section.

(f) Limit on dissemination. The Federal Bureau of Investigation may not disseminate information obtained pursuant to this section outside of the Federal Bureau of Investigation, except to other Federal agencies as may be necessary for the approval or conduct of a foreign counterintelligence investigation, or, where the information concerns a person subject to the Uniform Code of Military Justice, to appropriate investigative authorities within the military department concerned as may be necessary for the conduct of a joint foreign counterintelligence investigation.

(g) Rules of construction. Nothing in this section shall be construed to prohibit information from being furnished by the Federal Bureau of Investigation pursuant to a subpoena or court order, in connection with a judicial or administrative proceeding to enforce the provisions of this Act. Nothing in this section shall be construed to authorize or permit the withholding of information from the Congress.

(h) Reports to Congress. On a semiannual basis, the Attorney General shall fully inform the Permanent Select Committee on Intelligence and the Committee on Banking, Finance and Urban Affairs of the House of Representatives, and the Select Committee on Intelligence and the Committee on Banking, Housing, and Urban Affairs of the Senate concerning all requests made pursuant to subsections (a), (b), and (c).

(i) Damages. Any agency or department of the United States obtaining or disclosing any consumer reports, records, or information contained therein in violation of this section is liable to the consumer to whom such consumer reports, records, or information relate in an amount equal to the sum of

(1) $100, without regard to the volume of consumer reports, records, or information involved;

(2) any actual damages sustained by the consumer as a result of the disclosure;

(3) if the violation is found to have been willful or intentional, such punitive damages as a court may allow; and

(4) in the case of any successful action to enforce liability under this subsection, the costs of the action, together with reasonable attorney fees, as determined by the court.

(j) Disciplinary actions for violations. If a court determines that any agency or department of the United States has violated any provision of this section and the court finds that the circumstances surrounding the violation raise questions of whether or not an officer or employee of the agency or department acted willfully or intentionally with respect to the violation, the agency or department shall promptly initiate a proceeding to determine whether or not disciplinary action is warranted against the officer or employee who was responsible for the violation.

(k) Good-faith exception. Notwithstanding any other provision of this title, any consumer reporting agency or agent or employee thereof making disclosure of consumer reports or identifying information pursuant to this subsection in good-faith reliance upon a certification of the Federal Bureau of Investigation pursuant to provisions of this section shall not be liable to any person for such disclosure under this title, the constitution of any State, or any law or regulation of any State or any political subdivision of any State.

(l) Limitation of remedies. Notwithstanding any other provision of this title, the remedies and sanctions set forth in this section shall be the only judicial remedies and sanctions for violation of this section.

(m) Injunctive relief. In addition to any other remedy contained in this section, injunctive relief shall be available to require compliance with the procedures of this section. In the event of any successful action under this subsection, costs together with reasonable attorney fees, as determined by the court, may be recovered.

§ 626. Disclosures to governmental agencies for counterterrorism purposes [15 U.S.C. §1681v]

(a) Disclosure. Notwithstanding section 604 or any other provision of this title, a consumer reporting agency shall furnish a consumer report of a consumer and all other information in a consumer's file to a government agency authorized to conduct investigations of, or intelligence or counterintelligence activities or analysis related to, international terrorism when presented with a written certification by such government agency that such information is necessary for the agency's conduct or such investigation, activity or analysis.

(b) Form of certification. The certification described in subsection

    (A) shall be signed by a supervisory official designated by the head of a Federal agency or an officer of a Federal agency whose appointment to office is required to be made by the President, by and with the advice and consent of the Senate.

(c) Confidentiality. No consumer reporting agency, or officer, employee, or agent of such consumer reporting agency, shall disclose to any person, or specify in any consumer report, that a government agency has sought or obtained access to information under subsection (a).

(d) Rule of construction. Nothing in section 625 shall be construed to limit the authority of the Director of the Federal Bureau of Investigation under this section.

(e) Safe harbor. Notwithstanding any other provision of this title, any consumer reporting agency or agent or employee thereof making disclosure of consumer reports or other information pursuant to this section in good-faith reliance upon a certification of a governmental agency pursuant to the provisions of this section shall not be liable to any person for such disclosure under this subchapter, the constitution of any State, or any law or regulation of any State or any political subdivision of any State.

Legislative History

House Reports:
No. 91-975 (Comm. on Banking and Currency) and
No. 91-1587 (Comm. of Conference)

Senate Reports:
No. 91-1139 accompanying S. 3678 (Comm. on Banking
and Currency)

Congressional Record, Vol. 116 (1970)
May 25, considered and passed House.
Sept. 18, considered and passed Senate, amended.
Oct. 9, Senate agreed to conference report.
Oct. 13, House agreed to conference report.

Enactment:
Public Law No. 91-508 (October 26, 1970):

Amendments: Public Law Nos.
95-473 (October 17, 1978)
95-598 (November 6, 1978)
98-443 (October 4, 1984)
101-73 (August 9, 1989)
102-242 (December 19, 1991)
102-537 (October 27, 1992)
102-550 (October 28, 1992)
103-325 (September 23, 1994)

104-88 (December 29, 1995)

104-93 (January 6, 1996)

104-193 (August 22, 1996)

104-208 (September 30, 1996)

105-107 (November 20, 1997)

105-347 (November 2, 1998)

106-102 (November 12, 1999)

107-56 (October 26, 2001)

Endnotes:

1. The reporting periods have been lengthened for certain adverse information pertaining to U.S. Government insured or guaranteed student loans, or pertaining to national direct student loans. See sections 430A(f) and 463(c)(3) of the Higher Education Act of 1965, 20 U.S.C. 1080a(f) and 20 U.S.C. 1087cc(c)(3), respectively.

2. Should read "paragraphs (4) and (5)...." Prior Section 605(a)(6) was amended and re-designated as Section 605(a)(5) in November 1998.

3. The Federal Trade Commission increased the maximum allowable charge to $9.00, effective January 1, 2002. 66 Fed. Reg. 63545 (Dec. 7, 2001).

INDEX

A

Account Profile 47, 69
American Express 34, 88, 154, 157
ATM 41, 167, 168
authorized user– 112, 113, 173

B

bankruptcy xiv, 18, 35, 46, 47, 52, 59, 63,
　　　　69, 86, 88, 89, 90, 91, 104, 106,
　　　　109, 110, 118, 119, 121, 131, 136,
　　　　137, 138, 140, 141, 142, 145, 146,
　　　　151, 184, 185, 222
BEACON 51
Better Business Bureau 181
Blue Book 122
budget 100, 117, 131, 132, 133, 134, 135,
　　　　143, 144
business failure 19

C

capacity 100
car lease 122, 123
car loan 58, 74, 120, 121, 122, 128, 149
Chapter 11 109, 119
Chapter 13 63, 84, 89, 90, 109, 119, 137,
　　　　142, 146, 149
Chapter 7 62, 84, 89, 90, 109, 118, 137
Character 93
CHECKPOINT 47
co-applicant 108
collateral 16, 19, 20, 58, 86, 93, 102, 103,
　　　　106, 107, 127, 129, 130, 138, 139,
　　　　148, 149, 171, 172, 173, 174, 185,
　　　　261, 308, 309
collection agencies 21, 34, 80, 81, 116,
　　　　147, 185
Comments section 45, 68

community property law 114
confirmation number 44
Consumer Credit Protection Act (CCPA)
　　　　21, 26
consumer credit protections 21
corporation 104, 256
cosigners 108
Credit Abuse Resistance Education (CARE)
　　　　114
credit bureaus xiii, xiv, 30, 31, 32, 33, 34, 35,
　　　　38, 39, 40, 41, 43, 44, 48, 50, 51,
　　　　54, 59, 61, 64, 66, 67, 70, 71, 73,
　　　　79, 80, 81, 82, 84, 85, 86, 91, 92,
　　　　107, 108, 109, 112, 114, 118, 124,
　　　　150, 166, 173, 178, 182, 190, 191,
　　　　194, 195, 198, 200, 234, 235, 247
credit capacity 97, 100, 101, 255, 256, 264,
　　　　305, 307
credit cards xiv, 16, 31, 33, 50, 59, 87, 94, 98,
　　　　108, 111, 115, 132, 136, 137, 139,
　　　　141, 153, 154, 155, 156, 157, 158,
　　　　159, 164, 165, 166, 167, 168, 169,
　　　　170, 171, 173, 174, 176, 177, 178,
　　　　179, 182, 191, 192, 194, 198
credit file 21, 22, 31, 34, 35, 36, 37, 62, 76,
　　　　82, 105, 109, 110, 112, 117, 150,
　　　　175, 196, 220, 231, 238
credit line 50, 95, 96, 103, 110, 111, 158,
　　　　162, 168, 169, 170, 172, 182, 188
creditors xiv, 17, 21, 24, 29, 30, 32, 33, 35,
　　　　36, 38, 42, 43, 44, 46, 48, 50, 53,
　　　　60, 65, 67, 73, 74, 76, 78, 80, 82,
　　　　87, 89, 90, 93, 94, 97, 98, 99, 101,
　　　　102, 103, 104, 106, 110, 113, 114,
　　　　116, 117, 118, 137, 139, 141, 142,
　　　　143, 144, 145, 146, 147, 150, 151,
　　　　178, 188, 198, 223, 231, 242
credit report xii, xiv, 20, 21, 22, 29, 31, 35,

36, 37, 39, 40, 41, 42, 43, 44, 46,
47, 50, 51, 54, 59, 60, 61, 62, 63,
64, 65, 67, 68, 69, 70, 71, 72, 73,
74, 75, 76, 78, 80, 81, 82, 83, 84,
85, 86, 87, 88, 89, 91, 92, 93, 94,
95, 99, 107, 108, 109, 112, 113,
115, 116, 117, 118, 124, 146, 147,
150, 156, 165, 166, 190, 191, 193,
194, 196, 200, 206, 207, 208, 209,
211, 212, 213, 214, 215, 216, 217,
218, 219, 220, 221, 222, 223, 225,
228, 229, 230, 231, 234, 239, 241,
242, 243, 280
credit reporting bureaus– 30, 31
Credit scammers 181
credit score vii, xii, xiv, 18, 48, 51, 52, 55,
58, 61, 63, 87, 93, 94, 95, 96, 112,
115, 118, 124, 173
credit system xiii
Credit unions 119, 123

D

debit card 41, 171, 172, 173, 174
debt-to-credit limit 108, 111
debt-to-credit ratio 111
delinquent 23, 38, 42, 59, 68, 69, 110, 112,
116, 141, 149, 176, 211, 280, 321
delinquent accounts 59, 112
delinquent debt 110
Discover 34
discrimination 21, 26
divorce 19, 88, 151

E

ECOA 21, 29
EMPIRICA 51
Equal Credit Opportunity Act 21, 259
Equifax 30, 48, 50, 51, 52, 53, 71, 198, 199
Experian 30, 32, 40, 48, 51, 52, 53, 71, 177,
198, 200

F

Factual Data 124
Fair Debt Collection Practices Act 21
Fair Isaac 51, 54, 115

Fannie Mae 123
FCRA 21, 27, 36, 37, 44, 61, 63, 64, 65, 66,
67, 72, 76, 80, 185, 191, 222, 227,
236, 253
FDCA 21
Federal Trade Commission 73, 81, 83, 85,
183, 185, 205, 215, 226, 227, 247,
253, 267, 269, 270, 285, 291, 302,
312, 313, 316, 317, 334
Federal Truth-In-Lending Act 17
FICO 31
FICO score 31, 39, 40, 51, 52, 53, 54, 55, 58,
59, 93, 94, 95, 96, 108, 109, 110,
111, 112, 113, 115, 116, 123, 154,
156, 162, 165, 166, 169, 170, 176,
177, 178
foreclosure 45, 86, 131, 142, 146, 147, 149
foreclosures xiv, 34, 35, 42, 59, 62, 68, 88,
150

H

HAWK ALERT 47
Historical Status 44, 68
home equity loan 111

I

identity theft 19, 188, 197, 198, 199, 200,
201
Inc. 51
in dispute 23, 294
inquiry 35, 50, 51, 87, 106, 115, 166, 177,
217, 263, 273, 283
installment accounts 95, 96
installment credit 19, 20
Insurance companies 36
investigated 22, 23, 78, 184, 210, 215
investigative consumer report 23
IRS v, 36, 46, 63, 84, 86, 89, 109, 152

J

jewelry 19, 103
job loss 19, 141
Joint accounts 92
judgments xiv, 33, 34, 35, 42, 59, 62, 68, 84,
85, 88, 89, 150, 279, 303

L

lender 19, 20, 28, 52, 55, 56, 57, 59, 86, 87, 97, 99, 100, 102, 103, 105, 106, 112, 113, 124, 129, 138, 147, 148, 149, 150, 175, 190, 193
life insurance 83, 121, 122, 139, 188, 280

M

MasterCard 34, 153, 154, 156, 158, 170, 174
medical bills 19
Medical Information Bureau (MIB) 37
merchant cards 109, 170, 177

N

National Association of Mortgage Brokers 124
negative marks 20
non-installment credit 19, 20

O

open account 117, 335

P

P&L 45, 68
passbook savings 19
passport 77
Personal information 47
pre-tax income 100
profit and loss 45, 68, 69, 279, 280

R

Rapid Re-score 124
real estate 19, 29, 57, 102, 103, 125, 150, 171
red flags 35
repossession 46, 86, 106, 131, 142, 146, 149, 150
repossessions xiv, 35, 59, 62, 85
revolving accounts 95, 96
revolving bank credit cards 111
revolving credit 20, 111

S

SBA loans 129

Secured credit 19, 102
secured credit cards 108, 173, 174
secured loans 102
Small Business Administration (SBA) 129
social security card 77
social security number 31, 33, 40, 41, 48, 62, 71, 88, 89, 188, 193, 194, 195, 196, 197, 199
student loans 109, 334

T

tax liens xiv, 34, 42, 59, 62, 68, 106, 112, 131, 279, 303
Telecheck 199
The Equal Credit Opportunity Act 21, 26
The Fair Credit Billing Act 21
The Fair Credit Reporting Act ix, 21, 36, 214, 215, 253
The Fair Debt Collection Practices Act 21, 24
TransAlert 47
TransUnion 30, 32, 40, 48, 50, 51, 52, 53, 63, 71, 177, 198
TRW 32, 40

U

unsecured credit 19, 58, 168, 172, 173, 174
Unsecured creditors 102
utilization rate 95, 96

V

violations of law 23
Visa 34, 88, 153, 154, 156, 158, 170, 174

W

www.freecreditreport.com 54
www.myfico.com 54

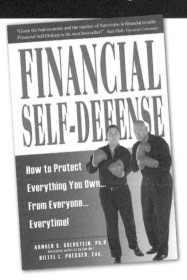

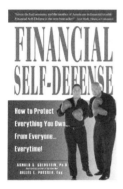

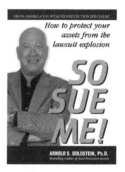
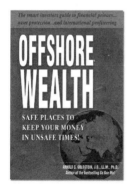

Invite one of America's top speakers to your organization.

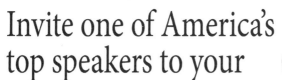

Arnold S. Goldstein, Ph.D. is one of America's top speakers on asset protection strategies... one of the hottest topics today. He promises an interesting, informative and entertaining talk on this and related financial topics before groups of any size and type.

Once he takes the podium, you are guaranteed fresh, innovative ideas, provocative wealth-preserving concepts, hard hitting "nuts and bolts" advice and the humorous touch that is the trademark of a Goldstein presentation.

A proven performer, Dr. Goldstein comes complete with a stack of recommendations and testimonials. But you can see for yourself, request a CD of one of his presentations.

For more information call
800-887-0748
or visit *asgoldstein.com*